I WOULD ALSO LIKE TO SAY THAT NO OFFENCE IS MEANT TO ANYONE READING THIS BOOK.

Run Of The Mill

By

Ed Chandler

Started in May 2009 and completed in September 2009

"Lif<u>f</u>E Is A Two Letter Word."

<u>I WOULD ALSO LIKE TO SAY THAT **NO OFFENCE** IS MEANT TO ANYONE READING THIS BOOK.</u>

This is not my first bit of writing and I hope it won't be my last…

This little bit here was an afterthought on the other hand, after I had already written this Run Of The Mill Book, and I guess I should first explain that I mean that as an informal title, as it is just a work of fiction that is nothing more than at times simply but "Run Of The Mill".

It amuses me that expression and there a lot of things in this book and the two that might follow, and well this rather amusing look at life through the eyes of a human is just Run Of The Mill…

So please do try to enjoy it…

Let me firstly say that I don't quite know how many times I will have to tell you that I'm sorry for any offence taken by anything in this book, but sometimes life is hard and we have to cope with hardship, it's just a part of life.

Should you be so offended by something in this book then unfortunately all I can do is apologise.

It is not my intention to offend you, but instead I'd rather try to get you to think about life in a different way to that in which you think of life now.

Some books start and they end with no one caring about them, you get to the middle and although you enjoy the book it is not what you expected, and I hope that this book will be the same.

NOT WHAT YOU EXPECTED!

Now if every book has a beginning, a middle and an end. Then what happens when we change the format? Do we upset the standard process of the book?

Should we always have the start, the middle and the end?

I mean if you knew that Romeo and Juliet died before falling in love, or why they were dead before they ever met, then you would want to read from the end of the book to the beginning?

You see having Romeo and Juliet dead at the beginning of the play is still going to be a good read.

Going back to front can be strange and unusual, but it can be quite entertaining. It is of course quite challenging and intriguing to begin at the end and have say for instance a dead body on stage, but not know the reason why the body is there, or who it is or how they died, this is often the case for Sherlock Holmes.

With anything that starts and ends quite normally or any book that tells you a story in the standard format of beginning middle and end. Well then, this is what I would call a "Run Of The Mill" book or novel or play….

And of these so called 'Run Of The Mill' books, the ones that take on the normal and abnormal. The romantic novels, sci-fi comics or murder mysteries. They are fiction in any form...

But we all love a bit of Fiction every now and then right? We all love a good 'Run Of The Mill' book every now and then, even if we don't tend to realise we are reading one.

        This is no 'Run Of The Mill' book, this is no novel.

Instead this is a book that will amuse you or confuse you. It has a few of life's little foibles in it and some of those silly questions we sometimes ask…

This book is about life in many different ways and how we use music, literature, the people we meet, the love we have and the work that we do to shapes our lives.

It will be like you wrote it yourself, only I did and now you're sitting here nice and comfortably, perhaps with a beverage of some sort.

Before going back to the start and going through the middle until the book is over we will have gone on a little rollercoaster ride of the brighter and darker sides to the world in which you and I live…

So if you are ready to start then we will begin with the chapters of this odd little book which are:-

The Weather

The Start Of It All

Teenagers

Music

The Middle

Lying

Living

Losing

Getting Ready To Go

When It's All Gone

These are the topics that we shall cover. Just do me one small favour please.

Remember one thing and remember who said it…

> "LifE Is A Two Letter Word."

Now then if you're ready, let's get down to the subject of…

The Weather.

Come rain or shine we all complain about the weather in Britain. Everyone does it, even the Romans complained about it when they were here.

So it's in our history, it is our nature to moan about how hot it is, or how cold, wet and miserable it is…

The thing that gets me is that when in the dark days of winter we long for those long hot days of summer. Once it gets to twenty plus degrees, suddenly it's too hot! We begin to wish it was cooler again! We are quite strange when it comes to the weather.

Like it or not but I think that as a matter of fact, British people just like to moan about the weather. I mean I have as of yet never known anyone else to have has many different types of rain as we do.

And this brings me to a subdivision within what I am sure you will find funny, hard to believe, or you will agree that you are one of those people who go on holiday to Sunnier climbs and then ends up ringing back home to see what the weather is like.

And if you are one of those people who thinks that the weather is an excellent topic for conversation, and what is more that no matter where you go… You always take the weather with you!

Especially the bad weather and that like I said brings me to an odd thing that we've done with rain. You see rain is not just rain any more, oh no! We have names for rain, we have as I am sure you will agree or disagree that in Britain we have:-

Many Types Of Rain…

"It's SPITTIN'… everybody in!" A line once said by Peter Kay and it was one of those things he remembered from his school days. And that's how most of the rain in this country starts for most of us. Rain begins by SPITTING about…

Sometimes however the HEAVENS just open up and then there is that SUDDEN Rain or the stuff that really DRENCH'S you! Rain that comes down so HARD, it hits the floor and bounces back up.

I don't know who first said that it was "Raining Cats and Dog's" But it's an odd expression, just like the fact that it would start to rain men all of a sudden.

Just like it won't rain chocolate or money, unless you had billions to just give away, so went into town, stood on top of a tall building and then poured the money on to the streets to give the impression that it was raining money...

So sadly whether it's PISSING it down or it's just that FINE DRIZZEL the stuff that soaks you right through...

Rain is Rain; I mean you get wet either way, right?

So if you're sat safe and warm inside and look out at the rain and realise your going out soon, then my advice is to put on some sensible footwear, a waterproof coat and grab the umbrella.

Then if it POURS it down or CHUCKS it down for that matter, come rain or shine and through the patchy weather we seem to get thorough quite alright...

Even when it goes gloomy and it gets all overcast and the storm clouds start to appear, don't run in fear, stop and just start singing in the rain...

Some people would even have soft, light, heavy and hard rain. Monsoon or Thunderstorm, moist or refreshing... Sometimes the weather will be fine, or it will be miserable and if I've missed out any particular type of rain that you know of or call out as the water falls from the clouds...

And well should your particular expression for RAIN not be mentioned then I do apologize. I just didn't want to waste time asking everybody I knew every time it was raining differently to the day before, what they called this particular type of rain...Sorry...

And besides if you're really clever then you'll know that the weather changes wherever you are. It's the same if you're at the coast in the glorious sunshine, yet just twenty, or forty miles away you can see the lightning and you can hear the faint rumble of thunder. You can be safe in the knowledge that the weather is just awful over there.

One last thing and I'd like to say that I thought of as I was writing this, but I didn't. It wasn't until I caught the weather report on television one night.

I was checking ahead to see what it would be like for the next day right, and by chance the Weather Person was right. There were sunny spells with SHOWERS.

SHOWERS? SHOWERS!? I thought Showers were found in bathrooms and you normally take off all your clothes in a Shower. I mean one of the silliest terms for Rain that I know of must be SHOWERS…. Right?

After all next time there is a Shower you wouldn't want to start stripping off, and then get some shower gel and proceed to wash yourself, I mean how daft can you get?

And so a Shower in the bathroom will never be the same as a Shower in the rain...

And that's why even though the words are spelt the same, I wonder if the invention of the shower was called a shower after the type of rain, or it was the other way around…?

I mean it never rains, but it pours, silly that…

I mean it has to rain at some point for plants and trees to grow. And the weather can never be the same all year round otherwise what would happen during summer and winter?

So then on a subject connected to the weather we have the seasons…

Whatever happened to those days when you were guaranteed a White Christmas, or a Hot Summers Day?

If you know Climate Change is happening, then more needs to be done to slow it down. Those that don't care won't and the world will be one big puddle.

When the Ice Caps have all melted, can I borrow your boat?

But for now the Sun is shining, and there is not a cloud in sight. So sit back and relax, for we've still a few things about the weather to discuss and fuss about.

I mean in between the rain and sun we have a whole new type of weather, we have MUGGY, HUMID or CLOSE?

I'd never heard of it being CLOSE outside before, but I've often said it was Muggy….

Weather is depressing, or happy, it has feelings apparently? Does the weather have the feelings, or is it us that get the feeling the weather will do whatever it wants to do, and unfortunately we can't really control it.

And then there are the seasons that are a part of the weather if you like, and we have this strange thing with the seasons, we expect nothing but sunshine in the summer, a cold winter, a wet autumn and a bright spring.

The calendar is shaped by the seasons, but not the weather, it could snow in the middle of June if it really wanted to, and I've seen snow in early spring.

It was on March the 23rd 2008. I woke up to see a blanket of snow across the ground. I had never seen snow in Lincoln as late as March, in the North Pole you get it all year round, maybe in Finland as late as early spring, but good old Lincoln?

And when the leaves are still clinging to the trees in November, maybe I should get rid of the Land Rover that does three miles to the gallon?

I'd just like to point out that I don't actually drive at this moment in time. That is today Monday 20th July 2009 at 15:30, and if you miss something this year then it will be at 12:34:56 on 07/08/09.

Now that is <u>12:34:56 07/08/09</u>, so at Twelve thirty-four and fifty-six seconds on the seventh of the eighth of this year two thousand and nine. It will be: **1 2 3 4 5 6 7 8 9.**

This won't happen for another thousand years, but most of us will have missed it by the time this book ever get's on the shelves.

My very best friend in the world Darren told me this, he's a real good friend and his partner Jo Clark to, she is an excellent cook, but I digress.

Back to long hot summers and dark cold winters, only when it's winter here it's summer in Australia, so you could have spring summer, spring summer all year round!

Go down under for Christmas and have a BBQ on the Beach, now that does sound like a good idea we should all take a….

HOLIDAY

Whenever we Brits go on holiday to a really hot country like Kenya or Cuba, Thailand perhaps or somewhere along the Equator. We never really expect that it will be as hot as we thought it would be when we get there.

Take the tale of the man who went to Cairo in July with an umbrella.

As the plane pulled up on the runway, it was a good six hundred or more yards from the terminal, no bus came along side to ferry the passengers from the Air-conditioned jet to the Air-conditioned terminal, instead you had to walk. And to the amazement of some passengers, there were two ambulances beside the short, but long walk to the terminal.

Why the two ambulances? Why the man with an umbrella?

Well, it was a nice cool twenty one degrees on the plane and twenty five in the terminal building, but outside at twelve noon, it was a staggering FIFTY Degrees…

And as you can expect, it was <u>so hot</u> that a few passengers were overcome by the heat and they fainted, but the man with the umbrella made it. A few others who had landed at this time of year and this time of day, those few natives and the strong or clever minded made it to. Some copied the man with the umbrella. They held their hand luggage or a newspaper over their heads to shade the hot sun off them.

You see the man with the umbrella knew it would be very hot and without shade, you would be under the full force of the sun. This made the walk from the plane to the terminal building a rather uncomfortable one.

So if you're planning a holiday, just remember that the song was not quite that right... You see you very rarely TAKE THE WEATHER WITH YOU.

If you want to enjoy your holiday, then do a bit of research, that's what the internets for. Look at the brochure, it sometimes tells you what the average temperature is for each month and the usual weather to be expected, but as anyone will ever tell you can hardly trust the Weather Person….

Even when they do get it right, the weather will change its mind, it will go from sunny to soaking wet and no one can do very much about it…

So we are stuck with the weather and we are all going to have to carry on smiling, when the clouds are grey and there is no hope of it brightening up for the Bank Holiday weekend…

And I tend to find that the weather goes wrong on most Bank Holiday weekends, instead of it being glorious sunshine we tend to get lumbered with wet and wild weather... Funny that…

It's not all the time! There are good weather days just as there are bad weather days...

I do hope I haven't bored you by talking about the weather first, but it's often the main talking point for any conversation, even when you're on Holiday. You'll find yourself ringing back home just to see what the weather is like, and the other person at the other end of the phone is guaranteed to ask you what the weather is like in your neck of the woods. If you haven't all ready told them, that is….

Talking about the weather is one of the things that makes us human, I'm sure that other animals don't talk about it, they most likely don't moan about it as much as we do, they just cope with it and so should we sometimes.

So whenever we watch the weather on television or listen to it on the radio, we will discuss the weather in any case just as when often we look outside to see what the weather is like. We have the safety of a roof over our head, we are dry, but outside it is wet, it rains, but how is it raining, how wet is it, will it dry up in a bit, or stop while I pop down the shops…

Silly questions like: 'Why is the THIRD HAND, on a watch called a SECOND HAND?'

It's daft I know and every now and then you'll get something daft like that in this 'Run Of The Mill' book..

For when it comes to the chapter about living later on, we see that often the weather will affect what we can do in life along with many other things, but as I was typing, I was thinking...

Well I thought that if it rains so much, well what about counting those rain drops?

And I think you'll see that if anyone took the time to count all the day's it rained, count every last millimetre that fell in your life time….

Well, what do you reckon? Would you have enough water to say…?

A: Fill up One Million Bath tubs

B: Re-fill the English Channel.

C: End the drought in a Third World Country. Or…

D: You don't actually know and neither do I.

And while we are considering things that will happen in our lifetime did you know that by the time you are eleven you will have took enough footsteps to get to China.

And I just wonder if some scientist, who should be trying to find better ways of curing Cancer will now rather instead investigate that very question, just because I asked it. They will try to work out how much rain has fell in their life thus far and if that is the case Mr or Mrs Scientist, I'd rather you find better cures for Cancer please, if it's all the same to you, it was raining yesterday, and I'm surprised it isn't today.

If the weather wasn't important then nothing else would be, would it?

It's not as if we need to know why it rains, anyone who can think back to Science or Geography might remember learning how water evaporates from the sea into the air and forms clouds. The build up of water into the clouds and add to this the moister in the air, with low pressure and all that science guff, you get rain…

Or do five guy's or girls dance around singing a song to make it rain?

I wonder if rain dances ever work. I mean that would be something to see, in the middle of the Sahara Desert, on the hottest day ever known.

You could say "Hey, Rainmaker person, could you magic me up some rain please?"

And in a few minutes a cloud begins to form, it gets cooler, and soon the single drop of rain is felt on the hand, then on the face. Slowly it get's quicker, wetter, and now it is raining…You jump up and down and shout hurry!

Until you realise, someone turned a sprinkler on by mistake…. You were on a football pitch in gloomy wet old England, and you couldn't go to the Sahara

Desert, because you've not yet got a passport, let alone the money for it, so you go inside, have a nice cup of tea or coffee and you sit down at the computer and write some silly daft things to go in your 'Run of the Mill' book....

And as we seem to be done with the weather for now, and I'll try not to come back to it later, but it is part of life and living, so look out for it there, not that it bothers us as teenagers or that much in our early years, except when we want some sunshine so we can go outside and play, but all it does is rain, so you ask to go play in the rain and all your parents say is "No!"...

Spoilsports! Playing in the rain, our going out after the rain stops to splash in puddles is great fun when you're just a little kid. Only when we get to thirteen it seems to have lost its appeal…

So I guess now we must move on as this is actually after all….

The Start Of It All

The real start of this 'Run OF The Mill' book is "The Start Of It All", just as in life we are born so is my book...

But is it at birth or is it turning thirty or forty that life begins?

I mean nowadays, by the time you turn eighteen, you have to look thirty just to buy your first beer, or other alcoholic drink, despite the fact that you got totally drunk on your fourteenth....

Can you remember that first encounter with the demon drink? If you're led to believe your mum and dad, they probably put rum or brandy on your dummy when you were a baby to try to get you off to sleep... I'm not saying mine did, that would be irresponsible of me, besides my dad's not exactly what you would call 'Run Of The Mill'... but then again many of them aren't.

And mum, dad or the parent in the house can seem like the enemy when you're grounded on a Saturday night, but you love them to bits when the wallet or purse comes out to pay for a new action figure, I guess that little girls will want something different to little boys...

One thing being male that strikes me as odd is something I picked up off a comedian, and that is that any man who gets kicked in the testicles will only ever want it doing once, for after all, in his opinion this is the most excruciating pain he can experience....

Where as a woman will give birth two or even five times, and they say that this is the most excruciating pain that women can experience... I mean go figure.

By the way I'm not sexist, I'm Heterosexual, and quite polite. I just thought that we ought to establish that as a man, I will for a few paragraphs have a one sided view of the world, so I'll ask one are two women their view of this world, what it is like to give birth and their view of MEN. Sorry guys, even if we were created first, we still have to live with them.

So you may ask guy's what is our view of women? Well considering that the average male is supposed to think about sex every three seconds, check his bollocks every two minutes. Which you have probably just done as I mentioned it, and consider that most heterosexual men will look at women with one thing in mind...

        "She's fit! I'd like to 'shag' her...."

However, there are a few men who are more interested in a woman for what she has to say, her job and so on and so forth, but it will probably end up with the two taking all their clothes off for a good thrashing about on the bed.

And sex is supposed to get better with age; unfortunately some brainy scientist has most likely already done the research for this instead of curing Aids…

And on that basis: -

A man's sexual prime is his late teens to his mid twenties, i.e. 18 – 25/26, and a woman's sexual prime is in her mid thirties to her mid forty's, i.e. 35-45

Now I'm not saying this is fact, but I did read it somewhere factual, I did not just internet it. I'm sure it's pretty close, and if you really wanted to know for sure by all means go ahead and check for yourself please.

I guess if you internet it then it may be quite funny, rude and hard to explain in a public library…

I once screamed Arghhh! In a public library and everyone just looked at me, I did the same thing on an airplane mid-flight and everyone joined in….

But yet once more I leave the topic of how Life begins, I mean I got side tracked by the difference between Men and Women, even in this modern world where we are supposed to be all equal, there is still a difference between Men and Women…

It's not just in the body, or the way we look, talk or act, but it's what we do, how we are… and no two are the same, unless your identical twins, or triplets. Then again I've known identical twins and I could easily tell them apart, I mean one had a beard and the other did not…..

Brothers are different from one another, as are sisters…

I have one younger sister, Kimberley and a younger brother, Stephen (Steve).

Were all different, and so are you! But what makes us different? I mean, I am a man and Steve is a man, the only odd one out if you like is Kim, because she is a girl, but then again we could be the odd one out to her.

So Men can look at women as cooks, cleaners, someone to bear their children, they look at women as sophisticated, cool, interesting, an object of desire, and when I asked my little brother Steve "How do you look at women?" His idiotic response was… "With your eyes you prick."

Not at all helpful, I couldn't really be bothered to explain what I was after so I left it at that and got on with it, but how do men really look at women, I mean there is the sexist view, the open minded view, the I must go and shag that view or the plain I can look but not touch view, because I have a wife view…

Just how many different views there are, I don't know. Sorry.

And how do women look at men, I guess partly in the same way. Some women look at men as security, an object of desire, and a tool to do those difficult jobs, a baby making machine? I don't really know so I'll ask some women and anyone else I can think of, but first a male view point of the opposite sex from Anthony a man.

"You can't live with them and you can't live without them, you can never understand their mind. A women is always in the right, they always like to get their own way I suppose.

Sometimes women can be more trouble than what they are worth.

A relationship can work on two bases, you both have to trust each other and work together as a team to build the relationship to be at its best, to stay intact.

A woman can replace the need or want to masturbate. Women can change your life <u>for better or worse</u>, some can make you happy and some will make you sad. Love is what makes you stay together."

A term sometimes found in the marriage vows comes up in that little insight,

<u>'For Better or Worse'</u>.

Marriage is I guess, having not yet got married, a joining of two people in love together, male and female, male and male or female and female. I mean in this day and age why some people still hate the idea of two people in love who want to be married, or share the rest of their lives together is fine by me, even if they are of the same sex, or it's a goat…

Then I thought that just for balance I'd better ask him what a woman would say about men…

"God knows, you'd need to ask one yourself."

So I asked my good friend Katherine to tell me how she viewed men, after all I want to be as fair as I can, and no doubt this will cause countless arguments between you and your partner if you have one, no matter what sex they are…

When I spoke to Katherine, she told me that she wouldn't necessarily look at a man's crutch in the same way that I would look at women's breasts…

Now I know that seems very sexist of me to be going around deliberately trying to look at women's breasts, but I must admit that the majority of heterosexual men tend to look at this aspect of women a lot.

After all a women's breasts tend to stand out more as it were, they come in all different shapes and sizes just in the same aspect as a man's penis does.

So do we as men look for the outline of breasts, while women will look for that bulge in the trouser department…..?

I guess it's hard to admit it, but a lot of us do it.

So while I was thinking about it I should really discuss The Start Of It All which is of course birth, and seeing that I have never given birth, as I am a Man… I thought it best to ask someone who had given birth…

Kimberley, my sister has got three children, Liam, Sacha and Charlie, I think she wants a fourth but it's probably a long way off in the distance yet.

So talking to her as a woman I asked her what was the process of Pregnancy was like?

"You're waiting… you feel sacred at first, for the first three months some things can go wrong, but after this you are in medical terms sort of safe until the birth.

As it got closer to having Liam and my other children I felt happy and excited. On the other hand if you were to go into labour without any nearby help, then you would panic. And if you are at home you feel safe waiting for an ambulance.

Your hormones play up on you during the pregnancy, like getting ready for the baby before it has even arrived.

There are many things to get ready, like bottle feeding and the nursery and other things to take care of.

Then just to get one more woman's view of men I asked Kimberley "So what do you think of men then?"

"Sometimes I notice men checking me out, as I check them out... Just looking at men you can't really say what you think unless you actually know them. It's like the saying 'You should never judge a book by its cover', but people generally do before they start to talk them and get to know the person that they are..."

In the many ways that women differ from men, I have discovered that we both enjoy certain things in life as well as having many things to fight and argue about, we all share at least one common Human nature of love towards other humans and sometimes animals.

One thing I must point out is that it was suggested to me that I tell you the age of each person who has given me their view point, so that the full age range was taken into account I guess.

Sadly as much as I would have like to asked two five year olds, a ten or twelve year old, a few teenagers and some people in their twenties to thirties, then the middle aged right through till the sixties and up to the nineties...

I just didn't have the time I guess, or I thought on one hand it did not matter as much as you may think, after all if you asked your Granddad his view of women, it would no doubt be different to yours, just as if your Grandma was born in 1935 and lived through the Second World War, then her view of men would be different too.

Just as I am sure my view of women will remain pretty much the same until I reach my seventies, and any grandchildren or great children that may come along will inevitably have a completely different view of women to me...

In fact a women from say the 1600's would get a surprise to see women of today, Men from as early as 1066 would probably fall about laughing or be in disgust to hear that a woman was equal to a man..

Times change, the car came and it may go, we landed on the moon, we got television, I mean if you told most kids of five to ten years of age that they had to work in a field instead of playing on the 'WEE' or PS Playboy?

Then they would probably cry and moan. Victorian children that went to school were only allowed and taught to use their right hand to write with, to be left handed was to be thought devilish...

Boy's as young as seven worked in coal mines and some as young as five or six cleaned chimneys, no matter how we look at it, time has changed and so I'm not going to say how old my friends and family were when I asked them to do me a favour. I'm going to see if you agree or disagree or if your thinking, actually my opinion or view of the opposite sex is nothing like this, but I wonder what someone else put. So I asked Darren, but before I managed to get my friend to talk to me I had to wait. And as of yet on Saturday August 15th 2009, I did not have the view of my friend, it was not until Thursday 27th August that I got a view point of women from him.

Now my reason for telling you this is that the comment you are about to read, took time to get, it took someone time to think about the questions I asked regarding women, and it will take time for you to read it, so I hope you enjoy it, laugh at it and do not take offence at it, after all men and women always talk about one another..

Here then is the view of my very good friend Darren about women.

"I don't tend to view women's bodies that much in the sense of sexual attraction, I do like nice hair, but I much prefer a good personality over looks. I think that in any relationship the fact that you can have a real meaningful conversation, you can express your feelings and opinions. You should be able to talk to one another without regret or pain.

I guess in any relationship there should be some sort of intellectual level and that you do not necessarily have the same views as one another all the time. It can be good to disagree on some things."

And that was all I needed from Him and from the other people I asked.
So I would like to say thank you to my friends, and if you ever meet them, or they are sat in a pub, library, café or on a bus and they see you reading this book, chances are they'll come over and tell you that they are in the book you now hold in your hands.

Fame it seems comes differently to men and women, just as relations between men and men can differ to that of women and women and to those of the opposite sex.

Now early life poses a small insight into something we will have all experienced throughout our lives. It is the relationships we have and who we have them with, so let us take a look at relationships.

Part One:

Our early relationships are with family and a small group of friends, it is not until our teens that we tend to venture into relationships with other people whom we may refer to as our "boyfriend or girlfriend"

And we'll come to Part Two of relationships later on, but first let us indulge in those early relationships, the one between us and our mum or dad… that of our brothers and sisters if you have any and then there are Uncles, aunties Grandmas and Granddads….

Relationships formed with a GP or School teacher may even come into it without much thought, especially if you're only five or seven. It is the way of life that we need certain relationships at an early age to prepare us for the ones we are going to have later on in life, and instinctively our relationships with Family members will undoubtedly change as we get older…..

So did you ever play kiss chase around the play ground or try scare off girls because they had 'lergies' and you didn't want to know, you just wanted to play war, or tig.

Trying to remember what someone would refer to as your first girlfriend or boyfriend is a bit tricky when you get to twenty-six, but I do know whilst I was still living on Newark Road, so I was at Junior school I had a girlfriend just a little bit older than me….

Now I should point out that the dodgy powers that be in the year 2009 decided to ruin the country, put us in debt and call most schools Academy's, whatever they're supposed to be, I unfortunately don't know…

I went to Infant and Primary, then Junior before finishing at High School, I had a few disagreements with the educational system, and I had some good times, and today I consider myself to be well educated in my things, sadly I've forgot a few bits, but I still recall plenty to enable me to live this little life of mine.

And before you say I've digressed, I haven't… I'm trying to say that LOVE when you eventually discover its many different aspects it's an odd thing to experience when you're only five or seven…

For instance at Five I loved a pet goat we had called Shera, but I didn't love that goat in the same way that I love my Sister and Brother, well maybe Steve… ☺

For Your Information, Stephen is a great little Brother, fun for winding up and playing jokes on, I generally fount that this was the role of younger siblings, for you to blame things on that you had done, or embarrass, or be cruel to… and on the other hand to share things with and play games with, have someone to talk to and help you out when you need a hand.

Sisters and Brothers, Mothers and Fathers, family is family, you have to love them and you can hate them if you really want to at times, but either way, right from the start of it all your stuck with them for life.

And relationships get complicated as we mature, they come quicker, faster and often we can have three or four all in week, a sexual relationship that just lasted the night and tomorrow we'll probably be moving on from it all only to go and find another relationship for the weekend.

So sexual relationships are of course never going to be the same as those of the relationships you have with your pet dog or cat. And the relationship with work colleagues may only ever extend thus far and not so much that you'd invite them to your thirtieth, but you're happy to invite family members, even the ones you don't really care for and rather wish you didn't have to invite…

So you see when you're just five or six and heading for that early age of thirteen, relationships are mainly focused for yourself on that of the role of Mum and Dad, Sister and Brother, Uncle, Auntie and Grandparents. Possibly you're Teacher at school, but most certainly the friends that you have through school until you move on and find new ones that it is…

Come the day when you find a person that you want to then have a sexual relationship with, relationships during the young period in our lives are really quite simple, and like I said "It isn't until a little later that they start to change"

And thus then is it per chance a good time to go on to the next chapter all about those fantastic, changing and cruel, horrible and harmonious teenage years.

Teenagers

13 PUBERTY…

14

15

Sweet …

16

17 Car Driving Time

18 <u>PUB!!!!</u>

19 The End

You might be now thinking, after going on about the start of it all and how we men look and think about you women and vice versa in many and often baffling ways, why on earth do we come to a chapter solely about teenagers?

Well, your teenage years are supposed to be you're most memorable, they are the years you learn the most, when things begin to happen, I mean, if you pass your driving test at seventeen, it will last right up until your seventy! How cool is that?

Also in this chapter will be 'Relationships Part Two'. The tale of why we find that after puberty and having learnt about sex and on top of it all discovering that the little boy or girl we once where is now gone forever, and that the person sat next to me is rather quite, well sexy….

I guess it'll be interesting to go in to it later on. But for now back to the bump and grind of this 'Run OF The Mill' book….

Because from turning twenty, all we have to look forward to is being twenty one and then getting older as we hit, thirty, forty, fifty and finally sixty, until at sixty-five we might be able to retire and say we are now senior citizens, can we have a bus pass please.

I mean the only two times you get a bus pass, unless you're entitled to one all year around every year… well those two times are in your teens and when you get to sixty plus…. Which is odd?

So I came to the nifty conclusion that the teenage years are the best of times and worst of times, even if you can persuade some adult to go to the locale shop to get you some fags, or a bottle of cider to get drunk and do silly daft things, that seem like a good idea, or fun and quite amusing…

Shaving peoples eyebrows off, or writing TWAT on their forehead… I mean that is to say that often as teenagers we did many a silly thing, well I know did even if you didn't.

I mean you must have got detention at school or stayed out past the time you were supposed to be at home and snook in without mum or dad knowing, only to be grassed in by little or big brother/sister the next day…..

I remember sliding down the banister at high school and falling off, I had to be taken to hospital, and got three days off school. I just couldn't be bothered to walk down the stairs I guess, after that they put bolts through the banister to stop you sliding down it; to this day they are still there all because of me…

I got drunk at sweet sixteen because I had some money from my little job I got myself and I mean what else are you supposed to do at sixteen with £175 a week, after giving mum a tenner or twenty quid for lodge, most of it then goes on booze, right?

Looking back I could have paid to learn to drive, or go on holiday more, I got my passport and went places, but not as much as I could have done.

And that's why we have this little insight to why teenager years or full of laughter and tears according to one old philosopher who recalls back to being thirteen and losing his virginity….

And after all most people will lose their virginity during their teenager years, they will have their fist intimate kiss, better than the one they had when they were five or seven.

There is also the fact that Britain after all has the current highest teenage pregnancy rate in Europe, what this has to do with anything right now, but it does beg the question that if you are going to have sex, at least where a condom..

Condoms after all will at least prevent pregnancy and the passing of sexually transmitted infections, look at this way, once your balls have dropped, or your first period has passed, and those breasts require a bigger bra, the last thing you want is to be ill through having sex.

Sex is a good thing, it should be safe so that you can enjoy it for everything that it is meant for, I mean just look at sex in the dictionary and then look at the fact that the first meaning is to describe your sex, i.e. MALE or FEMALE…

Its last description is that of sexual intercourse which has its own meeting all together.

So other than going through puberty you find that hair grows almost all over, and not only do you then have to shave it off, to find that it grows back again, I guess women find that waxing is a lot worse than men shaving their faces….

Being a teenager I didn't feel like a young child, yet I also did not feel like I was in my twenties…

Different things happen as we go through our teenage years, I mean you can get a Saturday job from thirteen, at fourteen you can have a glass of wine with your meal in a restaurant and go up to the bar for a soft drink, at fifteen your one year closer to gambling, by sixteen you get your national insurance card, you can ride a moped. By seventeen you can learn to drive a car, and at eighteen you can drink, providing you can prove you're old enough to do so...

My advice for when you turn sixteen is to get your Adult passport so that you can say, hey look I'm old enough... also you can get your provisional licence at the same time….

And so at nineteen you can be safe in the knowledge that your teenage years are coming to an end, you will have left school and possibly by going to University... A bigger sort of school, you may be working full time, or had a job for three years now.

You may have joined the army at sixteen and now your three years of basic training are nearly over, but no matter what twenty is not that far away and your probably looking forward to being twenty one.

I remember being twenty one, and from then on in I was twenty one every year until I got to a quarter of a century… 25…

When I was twenty one I got wasted, I went to Paris, London, Rome, Berlin, Warsaw and Moscow... I had fun, it was great… I loved it, but it soon ended when I got to twenty two………..

And that is the sad point of being a teenager, when you break up for the six weeks holiday the shops are already selling "Back to School" stuff a week before you broke up, the rain seems to just pour down because of my three miles to the gallon car… and all that CO_2 floating about….

I mean come on Mr Scientist, do something about that please, rather than try to grow meat or modify a tomato so it's the size of a football.

Even when the sunshine's out you'll get bored very quickly, and if your one of those teenagers that likes to go out and commit crimes, you should beware of the crafty copper who'll be out to catch you red handed.

Crime doesn't pay and ASBO's are not a fashion accessory, and the drugs don't work they just make it worse when what you really need is some TLC and a good laugh as your friend lies fast asleep from all that cider they drank, so you get out your camera take a funny photo or put shaving foam in their hand and then tickle their nose and watch as they scratch it, placing the foam right in their own face.

Something's we do as children will be funny and others will be sad, we will lose friends and we will make new ones, we will change schools, unless you're at an Academy now…

If you ask your mum and dad what was like to be a teenager, they will tell you it was nothing like what it is now, and the same will go for your Grandparents.

And that's it, because teenagers seem to be getting ahead of it, some twelve or even eleven year olds begin to act like teenagers even before they get to thirteen. Grandma and Granddad were not like this, I'm in my twenties, and I'm sure I wasn't a teenager until I turned thirteen.

And this brings me to a daft point, say you are born early in the month say from the first to the tenth, then turning your age on the same number as they day comes quite early, and it comes later if you were born say on the thirty-first….

And after that there are no more days in the month. Unfortunately you cannot be forty on the fortieth day because there isn't a fortieth day.

But imagine being Thirteen on Friday the Thirteenth, or seven on the seventh of July nineteen seventy seven… at seven minutes past seven in the morning…

Now that would have been cool, if you could say I was twelve on December twelfth at twelve minuets past twelve at exactly 12 seconds past the minuet on the twelfth of December in the year 2012… So in effect that's six twelve's….

Impossible maybe, but what if it was long ago, like in 1212… years like 1111 and 1234 have already passed us by sadly, but others like 2121 and 5678 are still to come…

If any mathematic is quick enough to work out how many years will have passed from it being 1234 to 5678 then I would love to know, because I'm not that clever to try to figure it out….

But using a calculator it is of course exactly four thousand four hundred and forty-four years. So that's 4444, a year that will have been and gone by 5678… Blimey!

From AD zero it must have been daft to work out what it would be like come the first millennium at 1000… and now here we are in 2000 heading for three, but it'll take a long time to get there… As we go through the noughty's, twenties, thirties, forties and fifties. Through the sixties, seventies and eighties until the nineties the years will pass, the decades will be forever the same numbers, but life back in the nineteen twenties was nothing like that of the eighteen twenties and the same will go for the twenty twenties…

I don't quite know what they call the decade from ten to nineteen, perhaps the teenies? Or ten's?? Anyone know?

Again I could check, but you'll find something's in this 'Run Of The Mill' book are inspired to allow you the reader to try and discover for yourself, after all the recommended reading age for this will start from thirteen, so that all those level headed or half-witted teenagers will be wondering why should I care now about what I will be doing in just five or seven years time…

A question you might find that you will ask yourself the first time you see the careers advisor.

The careers advisor is here to tell you that now in your teenage years you will get the skills required to live out there in the real world, away from mum and dad, a world where you need to work, only at present there are barely enough jobs for those who are already in work, let alone the unemployed.

You will discover that the jobcentre is a devious place, a place that you will lose your temper with when your money does not come through, and when you forget to obey the rules are show up for something they wanted you for, you'll lose your money any way….

Working, drinking alcohol legally, smoking, shagging and generally growing up are all about to take place and all you really want to do is either:-

A: Enjoy the Sunday roast Mum just made.

B: Stay in Bed another hour, after all it's the weekend….

C: Get up, get ready and go out in to town with all your pals…

D: None of the above. Play on the 'Wee' instead.

But while we are on questions for a tiny second may I ask:-

If peanut butter cookies are made from peanut butter, then what are Girl Scout cookies made out of?

Don't worry I've got plenty more daft things to say and ponder; otherwise this would just be a 'Run Of The Mill' book, would it not.

Now nobody said it would be easy, but then life never is when you're a teenager.

And this brings me to another change in those teenage years, sexual relationships are often formed in the teenage years of our lives, after all it is the time in which we will have already passed through puberty by the time most of us are fourteen, and puberty can begin as early as eleven or twelve in girls, the breasts begin to develop and grow, just as a man's penis get's bigger, so do women's breasts.

Now I don't want to sound sinister, but you have to recall yourself that changing if not a little scary, but if not a bit embarrassing. I mean I'm a man, but if I were a women, and my boobs were suddenly to go from nothing to a size B or DD in the space of a few weeks, I'd be worried for a split second until I realized that they were supposed to do that.

So what about that first period? Again having not been born a girl, I can't say what it must have been like, and I guess you wouldn't really want to be sat here reading about it now if you were a man, but what if you were a woman?

Don't worry just to be clear, I think for the reason of shear disgust in the matter of describing what happens during the menstrual cycle to you, I think I'd rather not, I learnt about it in biology and even in sex education, we learnt about how we men and women were to differ as we passed through and finished puberty.

I guess now a woman should think to herself ok, what if I was man, and I woke up one morning and my penis was all hard and straight up, it was in effect fully erect.

I mean girls you must have noticed how men past the age of fourteen often check there balls by having their hands in their pockets, and it starts from an early age. It's the curiosity of what on earth is this dangly thing right in the middle between my legs?

I don't think girls do the same, do they? I mean sadly you've got no dangly bits as it were until you breasts begin to droop… Is that unfair?

So let us then very briefly talk about SEX:-

For a start I should point out that the LAW says that two person's consenting to have sexual intercourse must both be at least sixteen years of age.

Now if you are say fourteen or fifteen and in a relationship at present and wish to have sex with your partner, I might suggest you wait, there are other things to do.

I'm not going to say what, as I don't really want to encourage persons under sixteen having sex, or breaking the law in effect. So without spoiling things let's move on and look at the fact that being a virgin does not make you any more or less a person.

Your Virginity is quite special in a way, as it is one thing that once gone can never be replaced. It cannot be taken more than once, it is not something to throw away for the sheer hell of it and if you misuse it the first time you have a sexual encounter it will be something you regret.

Sorry to be Frank, but sex is a risky subject in our teenage years, it comes with many pitfalls, including the possibility of Aids, hepatitis, Chlamydia, and other sexually transmitted infections. The risk of pregnancy if no protection is used during your sexual encounter, so please be safe guys and girls use a condom, they are if considered a life saver really.

On the basis of a man and women having sex for the first time, losing your virginity may heart a little, after all the man is going to insert his fully erect Penis into your Virginia.

It is how ever quite an experience, if you have already had sex then you'll understand what I am talking about, just as is if I mention blow-jobs or the 69 position, 'doggy' or letting the woman go on top lads.

Sex is another thing that we humans do rather differently to any other animal on the planet, we have to flirt and woo our opposite sex for their attention, our if you are not in to the opposite sex but the same sex then it's still a question of approaching a possible 'mate' and trying to impress them into bed, or how ever you do it.

Each human I am sure has a different tactic of getting someone to have sex with them, providing you both want to then it's all right, sex should never be forced upon anyone, that is wrong…

So I think that's about it on sex and in a way I've sort of covered relationships part two…. No honestly I have, think about it. Your relationship with your parents has changed from when you were five to when you turn fifteen.

You don't want your parents to embarrass you, or show you up in front of the boyfriend or girlfriend, if your still at home when you are sixteen/seventeen and you have a partner and you are in a sexual relationship then you have to try and get the house to yourself occasionally or get in late with said partner for a night of passion.

Your parents are concerned for you to be having sex, a concern never raised before, they are worried that you stayed out all weekend, but you don't care, it was fun, you had fun, and what do they know, they are old…

It is the way of most teenagers, they like to think they are grown up before they get to twenty, when in fact they still have a lot to learn about this thing called life before they even get to twenty-one.

So what happens if you yourself become a parent at say sixteen or heading for nineteen? Is this then not the end of all those fun and exciting years you could have had, are your chances of going to university gone?

I mean I don't have children as of yet, but I guess at so young an age, the gift of a child, the creation of life could be joyful, daunting, and a little bit scary, but then hopefully the father will be around, mum and dad to support you as well as any older sisters or brothers.

I am an Uncle to three lovely children that my sister had from her late teenage years to her early twenties. She loves her children very much. I think they are great, you can teach little children so much, spoil them with chocolate and other goodies, but best of all hand them back to mum or dad when they smell. Nappy change Mum!

Kids go from so young to immature stages to early adulthood to actually becoming an adult rather quickly but actually over many years, twenty-one to be exact….

That is to say that most people regard the age of twenty one to be the best of all years in their life, it is an age we all look forward to and some wish they could go back to, or that they never left.

I mean sometimes it can be a bit predictable when a book about you're teenage years is just like everyone else's, and if all books are supposed to just have a beginning, middle and an end and that's it…Then why should your teenage years be the same?

Next time you read your favourite book bear this in mind. You know the beginning and the middle and you even knew the end. Ask yourself would you watch Star Wars if you knew Darth Vader died in the end, and he was Luke's father? Not a lot of music in the Star War's films…

And Music oddly enough is the subject we shall be discussing next. We will have come to it at some point as will television, film, literature and the people around us who we have many different relationships with.

But let us end these teenage years and discus…

It was my first love and it will be my last…

The first thing I should point out that, so as not to infringe on copyright, some lyrics from songs will only be quoted, the artist and particular songs mentioned. This is on the basis that I may recommend you listen to a certain song by an artist, and I encourage you to do so legitimately.

Also I have no intention of wanting to promote any song I mention, this would mean paying for the use of the song, and I do not need the use of the song, just the fact that for instance "Bohemian Rhapsody" by "Queen" is one of those tunes we should have all heard at some point thus far in our lives, and if you haven't yet, then I suggest you do….

I would hope that any lawyer would permit the mention of a song and the artist who originally performed it or the version I have personally heard. I don't think I need say more, so get your C.D collection ready as we explore music and what it means to you….

One of the great questions I heard posed by song was "What's that coming over the hill, is it a Monster?" A lyric from the song "Monster" by "The Automatic", now you may say that this is a strange place to begin with music, but often we miss odd lyrics like in a favourite tune of mine by "The Waterboys"…

"The Whole Of The Moon" is often played on Lincs F.M, my local radio station, and as the song goes on a little bit there is a line about "Unicorns and cannonballs"

So you see it's worth noting that some old songs and even some new ones sometimes might have a naughty word in them or one of those lyrics you miss-hear…

A perfect example of this was the song by Girl Band "The Saturday's" called "I Just Can't Get Enough". Now when you listen to that line, the last part sounds like, "an ouf"...

An '<u>ouf</u>' which is French for '<u>egg</u>'. So effectively the band was saying 'It just couldn't get "an egg"'… But we all know that is not the real lyric, this is just how it was miss heard by someone, even me perhaps…

So how about listening to some of this music? I'd like to give you a perspective of what is to come, I am an ecliptic... That is to say I like a full range of Music, I have the theme from "A Bridge Too Far" and I like some hard core tunes to, but mainly anything eighties… I enjoy some sixties, seventies and nineties tunes as well as some from today…

From Elvis Presley to Michel Jackson, through Abba and Queen to The Beatles and Simply Red, Prince, Eurhythmics, Bonnie Tyler and Tina Turner right back to Boyzone and The Veronicas.

So you can see that if you listened to say "Little Bird" by Annie Lennox or "Purple Rain" or "Gold" by Prince, then you'll see that there is always going to be some music you love and some you hate. I happen to like all of those songs I just mentioned.

A person who likes Mozart will most likely not listen to Guns and Roses, just as not everyone likes Elvis, I'm not too keen on Rap or Classical music, but I do have Enya's "Orinoco Flow" on my X-box with the rest of my collection of Music…

So try listening to Simply Red's song "Money's Too Tight To Mention" when you don't have a lot of money, or Tina Turner's "Ask Me How I Feel" for when you want someone to realise How you actually feel.

Certain songs do this for me, they portray the way I feel, they cheer me up and can easily pull me back down, "<u>Sad Songs</u> say so much..." <u>Elton John.</u>

Leo Sayer with "Words" that did not come easy to him and they often don't come easy to me, but words are what make us Human, no other animal has words… I mean have you ever heard a dog say hello, I know some Parrots can talk, but not like a full conversation… can they? No…I don't think so.

And songs from Films are some of the ones we tend to forget too, like in Bugsy Malone, Michael Jackson sings "We could have been anything that we wanted to be" in the final song "You Give A Little Love" right at the end of film as all the boys and girls have a huge messy fight with flour and cream pies.. Fantastic!!

Now a song that should really inspire you as at inspires me is "You're The Voice" by John Farnham, it begins:-

"We have the chance to turn the pages over. We can write want we wanna write"

And then later on:-

"We're all someone's daughter; we're all someone's son."

Which is part of the chorus, as is this:-

"You're The Voice try understand it, make a noise and make it clear…"

"We're not gonna sit in silence! We're not gonna live with fear!"

It is then in my opinion a brave song, that tells us all not to let people bully us, to stand up and be counted, to be recognised, and looked upon with respect. Well done to you John Farnham.

Now moving on to Films, because Films have some great Music in them, often without words, music helps to add drama, and to the mood of the film, for instance in the James Bond Films, often the James Bond Theme is played in action sequence's….

JAMES BOND: "Simply The Best."

"The Best" by Tina Turner who also sang "Goldeneye" did sing a great song, but Shirley Bassey who sang three Bond Movie songs, "Goldfinger, Diamonds Are Forever & Moonraker." Has to get the credit for doing the most for Bond Film Songs, after all most of us know that Goldfinger is the film, the Austin Martin DB5, Oddjob, and Pussey Galore, but it just wouldn't be the same without that opening Bond song.

Moonraker is my favourite Bond Film for anyone who would like to know, I should point out that I am also a huge Bond fan at this point as I sure he'll crop up again…

Madonna's "Die Another Day" and Lulu with "The Man With The Golden Gun" or Tom Jones with "Thunderball" all great Bond tunes, but…

"Nobody Does It Better" is of course Carly Simon's classic from "The Spy Who Loved Me"

And so I end with "A View To A Kill" by Duran Duran, and I am happy to admit I did side-track myself from the main subject of Music to discuss the Music of James Bond Films...

But we need to look at this area of Music as it covers Six Decades thus far, with the arrival of Daniel Craig in "Casino Royale". What we see is a variety of music, different types of music, from rock to pop and even a bit of classical, after all if you listen to the very first Bond Film song, "From Russia With Love", then you'll note that Matt Monro sang it, and compares not to the rhythm or tempo of Garbage's "The World Is Not Enough".

So music has changed as we have changed, from Mozart to modern jazz to pop and rock. Club music that often just sounds like a very loud noise, that gives you a headache after a while, or songs that just have no real rhythm or tempo at all.

"Nothing is so good lasts eternally, perfect situations must go wrong! But this has never yet prevented me wanting far too much for far too long."

A lyric from "I Know Him So Well" by Abba or redone by Steps…

Terry Jacks sang about "Seasons In The Sun", Annie Lennox asked "Why" Boyzone said "No Matter What" and Bryan Adams declared that "Everything I do, I do it for You."

Music is the best thing this modern world has, forget the car or internet, disregard the television, even though we can appreciate Music through them all, it's better to just sit at home and crank up the volume and have a little sing along if the mood takes you.

From the birth of pop through rock n' roll to early punk and house, the last fifty years or so has seen Music take on a whole new meaning, I mean if I had been born in 1066 or 1775, then Music would not be as it is now, there would be no Music videos, or something's like the electric keyboard. There were pianos in the 18th century, and violins or other string instruments as far back as 1066, not to mention drums or other instruments.

I don't want to focus too much on instruments, as I don't yet play any, I'd love to play the piano, but I think I may have left it too late to learn, but we shall see. After all you can often do anything when you put your mind to it.

So back to the classics, for a twenties guy would not listen to 'The King' and it is the same for those Vikings, for any drum and base, would be a disgrace…

So let's look at opening lines from some popular rhymes… sorry.

"All my life I've been waiting for you to bring a fairytale my way, been living in a fantasy without meaning. It's not ok! I don't feel safe…."

That is the opening line of "Left Outside Alone" by Anastasia. A great tune and opening lines often make us turn up the volume when the radio is on, we recognise the first few bars of music, we hear those first few words and it's perfect…

"Well it's hard to be a gambler, bettin' on the number that changes every time…"

Elvis Presley and the first line from 'Moody Blue', it's a song about a girl and we'll cover how songs relate to different things in life, like some will talk about men and some about women, 'Moody Blue' is based on the female, but "Gimme, Gimme, Gimme" by Abba is about a woman after a man.

'System Addict' by Five Star is a song about work, it is also a song that is quite appropriate for the computer age and all of us on Facebook instead of typing out reports or doing spreadsheets, don't worry, I love Facebook, feel free to add me.

'Come Back And Stay' by Paul Young could be either for a man or a woman it all depends how you listen to it, it is after all asking someone to come back into your life.

'Overload' performed by Alfie Zappacosta is definitely about a woman, it's a song that I did not really notice at first, I looked it over in favour of 'She's Like The Wind' by Patrick Swayze… but if you have the film Dirty Dancing, or the soundtrack, go put it later. And for now grab a cup of tea, get comfy and carry on reading until the end of the chapter.

Deacon Blue with "When Will You Make My Telephone Ring" I mean you may have heard "Dignity" or "Real Gone Kid" but the other one? Perhaps not, but then you may not have heard of Deacon Blue, so in that case now you have, and I can't force you to listen to those songs are any I have suggested thus far.

Remember that "If I tell you to do something and you don't want to, then you don't have to!"

Only consider this, I'd happily listen to any of your music, if I did not like it, or it was not to my taste, I'd simply say sorry, but have you got any "Queen"…

We all have different tastes in music, it's a good thing, just as we are all different, even twins, remember….

So what of Love, there must by music to make love to, or music that inspires love, talks about love and tells us that often it all falls apart, but one song that springs to mind is by Heart it's called "All I wanna do is make love to you."

Quite a straight forward title to be honest, great tune to by the way. I'm probably going to say that a lot, that this is a great tune, or that is a great tune, so you'll just have to grin and bear it for a bit more, I've got to bits in films and story's that you have to cringe at as you wonder where this is going, trust me, you didn't have to write it so, excuse me a second while I try to get back on track…

Some songs start with the title like "I Just Can't Help Belivin' " by Elvis Presley, or they have the title in the first line like 'The Motown Song' by Rod Stewart. After all "I've been meaning to tell you, I've got this feeling that won't subside. I look at you and I fantasize." Is the start of 'Hungry Eyes' also from the film Dirty Dancing, it was sung by Eric Carmen.

"Amazed" by Lonestar is a good love song, as is "Total Eclipse Of The Heart" by Bonnie Tyler, but my favourite is The Beatles and "All You Need Is LOVE"….

I mean after all I thought all I needed was the air that I breathe, or food, music and a few other things, but if all I needed was love….

If you took my life and made it complete, I would be happy, just as I hope anyone in love is happy. But you should have seen by the look in my eye, and told by the words that I said that music is one thing we can use to escape, it may talk about the weather and it may get more modern than you are used to, but the music you enjoy will last forever.

After all not many people go about forgetting them now, and for good reason, it's hard to get by when your arse is the size of a small country, and if you've not cottoned on just then, I'm saying nothing, I'm just leaving it all to chance and if the winner takes it all or we find ourselves in Nutbush City on a Saturday night with a bottle of bud and something inside so strong, then it might just be the music that will make sense of it all…..

I guess I closed my eyes, and you closed every door… "Joseph" I love that song where you sing all the colours of his amazing coloured coat, I mean just how many colours were there? But most of us may have been in Joseph at school, learnt about it, sang the songs and we all loved it secretly…

Anyone want a stroll down memory lane with those words again? "I closed my eyes, drew back the curtain…." Come on "Any Dream Will Do" Right?

It's one of those crazy songs like "Queen's" Innuendo, or "Barbie Girl" by Aqua, "Agadoo" or "The Music Man" by Black Lace, there are the songs that we have all enjoyed, but don't often admit to…

And often in a land of make believe, there are lots of songs we have, that we get very little time to take notice of, and there are the ones which we just listen to over and over again, I bet if you were asked to you would happily sing a little bit of your favourite song… especially if the person offered you five pounds to do so…

For me I would either try to sing "Little Bird" or "No More I Love You's" by Annie Lennox

The thing with "No More I Love You's" is that it begins quite unusually… It goes:-

"I used to be lunatic from the gracious days. I used to be woebegone and so restless nights. My aching heart would bleed for you to see. Oh but now. (I don't find myself bouncing home whistling buttonhole tunes to make me cry)"

Very odd but very cool, however you want to take it, but I like it, I mean I am strange, that's a certainty, but then I find it better to enjoy life then let it just drag along, otherwise there wouldn't be much point in being here.

"There's no point in living if you can't fell alive." A quote from the James Bond Film 'The World Is Not Enough'. Pierce Brosnan starred as Bond, and sadly it was the last film to feature the original 'Q' played by Desmond Llewelyn who was the replaced by John Cleese, who was called 'R' in "The World Is Not Enough", but he was 'Q' in "Die Another Day".

Sorry, but I did say I was a James Bond fan, and I like everything about it, but I like music a bit more, at least I think I do…

I still have room in my heart for more and although I don't want to fill it up, I still want to be able to enjoy all the things I enjoy about music. I enjoy the rhythm the soul, the mood it creates, it lifts, it empowers and drives me, it can upset me are bring me to smile for a while, but Music after all is a wonderful thing, no matter what life may bring.

To live without my music would be impossible to do, because in this world of troubles my music pulls me through.

And when it comes to those songs about an earlier chapter… The Weather, we have quite a few, just as people sing about love and men or women there are unfortunately songs about RAIN, with a few more focusing on Christmas. Yes music has taken on the seasons. I mean you can't listen to "Last Christmas" by

'Wham' on a hot summers day can't you? Well I guess you could in Australia, as there summer takes place in December, when it's Christmas…

So we have songs such as this, which we put on at a particular time of the year, but we have others that you can play anytime, and others that you just need to play regardless.

So I wish it would rain down on me for a second while I indulge the side of music I tend to play at just the right moment….

One of those songs is "Desert Rose" by Sting/The Police, or "Bat Out Of Hell" by Meatloaf, "Ask Me How I Feel" or "The Best" by Tina Turner. "Underground" by David Bowie from the film Labyrinth. "Invisible" by Alison Moyet, "Your Mirror" by Simply Red and "Lost In Space" by The Lighthouse Family.

I love to listen to music and some songs are better than others, a really good song has good lyrics. The words and music working together in perfect harmony, to make music just get better….

"The Promise" by 'When In Rome' Is I'm guessing a tune you'll not have come across, and I know some I'll have not come across too, some that you could mention, after all to take all the music in the world there must be what at least enough songs to go around the world a few times….

"The Time Is Now" by Moloko is where I'm going to end my joy of music, for now is the time me thinks to change tactics and begin a new chapter in this, now what was it, oh yes that's right it was a 'Run Of The Mill' book I was trying to write….

Let's leave this behind then, and let's head for….

THE MIDDLE

Or should that have been "The Middle?"

I wonder if that should have been posed as a question.

Perhaps not as the correct title is just simply meant to be: - The Middle

And sadly, I've no clue as to what the picture is, I just used clipart, typed in "The Middle" and that is what I got. So I apologize if it represents something other than 'The Middle'…

What Fun I'm having writing this 'Run Of The Mill' book, only now I'm stumped for a bit, and my bum's gone numb, so it's time for a good cup of coffee and a lemon puff, or piece of shortbread…

Sometimes it's a question of empty pages waiting to be filled, like an empty life without cause, IF only life was simple….

Now nobody said it would be easy for me to write this book, and if you ever decide to sit down and write one, think long and hard first about it, I did and look where it got me… 'Run Of The Mill'

I just said the title of book twice granted, but we are now half way through, so is it all downhill now? Is that life? Is that music? All good things come to end, right?

Well that's what we are going to try to work out now, what the middle actually is, or what it means to you, just as the grand old Duke of York had ten thousand men, he marched them up to the top of a hill…and then marched them back down again…

When they were up, well they were up, when they were down they were of course down, but when they were only half way up, they were not only neither up or down, but they were in the middle!

And where is the middle in certain places like the universe our earth, I mean there is a place called "Nowhere" in America and a sign that says "You are now in the middle of Nowhere." I unfortunately have never been there, but I know someone who has, I think that's pretty cool, to actually be in the middle of nowhere…

If this 'Run Of The Mill' book had a beginning, and it will end at some point, and I'm saying that this is the middle, wouldn't it be daft to begin here, or even end here… Often we rely on their being a start, the middle and an end to most things in life, including life it's self of course.

Middles are at thirty and forty, or as late as fifty in the term of having a mid-life crises, and if you read this book in order and your just a teenager, then I guess a mid-life crises is something to look forward to, right?

And then again, I guess it isn't, I mean I'm only twenty-six, so I'm quite some time away from having a mid-life crisis… At least I hope I am. I mean is there such a thing as an early mid-life crisis?

And why do the 'Slow Children' signs have a picture of two running children?

Again a daft question at the wrong moment, it's not too through you off, it's to stop and make you think, use some of those grey little brain cells in the back of your mind.

I mean I like the bit on the back of most books that gives you an insight to the whole novel of affairs that is about to take place when you start at the beginning of the book. Normally at the back there is a picture of the author and a little bit about them, this is often the norm in most books, but not this 'Run Of The Mill' book, no I stuck to tradition…

Bugger! Silly thing to have done there by giving away the key to the plot, but by now you should have realised that this book has not got a hot plot to it. This book is strange and compelling, full of the things we often take for granted and things we never realise, but they occur to us all in 'LifE'.

We always miss the most important things when they are gone, we never take the time to appreciate what we have got, we waste so much time and time is often precious to us all.

Sleep, work, love, life and the little hiccups that come and go are way. We could get married, we could have children, we could be working, we could be Disabled or suffer from some underlying illness for years until it finally kills us, and no one will have ever been any the wiser.

Death which we will come to later is now a little closer, it is still a long way off by any means at forty, but if you only live to eighty, then you're half way there…

Some scientists can work out roughly at what age you will die, and that's a bit of an unusual thing to know if you were only twenty-something when they tell you. If I had the choice in being able to know at what age I was going to die and not knowing, then I would rather not know…

Sometimes in life you will have to deal with idiots, and daft twats. They come in many forms, bullies and clowns… Not circus clowns, but the fool's. They can be so naive, and petty, they think they are having fun, they do not care about you really, you are just a laugh to them, you are a game, and sometimes you have to get the upper hand.

It can be tricky, but it is rewarding, it is not a case of revenge, it is not that you have to use while and cunning, but it does mean doing something's that you would not normally do.

In the Middle of things, especially war, it can seem as everything is going slowly, like in the films, it all slows down for a split second, but it soon passes you by very quickly…

Faster than the speed of night or a bullet from a gun, in the middle of it all, where are we exactly?

When we start to think about getting older as we are all certain to do, it should never get you down, in fact getting older is just a natural part of life, and it is meant to happen, just as sure as death will happen.

Any middle of any life should be great, it should be more memorable than those teenage years, it should be the time that if you have a family, you enjoy the time you have with them. If your children are getting old enough to be starting a family themselves, and then becoming a Grandparent as early as thirty to forty should be rewarding too.

If I become a Grandparent at forty then I would be happy, after all it's something to celebrate in my book, being a Granddad…I just can't imagine it right now, or being a Great-granddad for that matter. But I guess Life does change, and I will of course change.

Remember when you do something it can be like throwing a stone into a still, calm like. The stone hits the water and the ripples spread from the point of impact. Actions can be similar, they hit our lives hardly and the ripples have a knock on effect.

As we go along with our lives, if something happens, we can reflect upon it. Recall the happy or sad moment. If you kept a diary for a month, or a year. Day by day, then there would be high's and there would be low's.

I just don't know why we do some of the things we do. Hurting one another, so that the other hardly recovers. Love that is so cruel and yet so kind. The twist and the turns of the human mind. A maze, a riddle, the greatest puzzle of them all is LIFE.

>You've got to love it or you've got to hate it.

Life is a game with laws and rules that you can bend or brake, cheat or not. You're the one who has to live with the decision you make and the consequences of that decision.

Is your life a chosen path that you must follow, or one that you can change? Does the path twist and turn so that if you go left, right, or straight on, but never back…

What if you could go back? If the choice is which way to go, and all choices have an effect on where you'll end up. But then again what happens when you get to where you wanted to be?

Does anyone have the answer? I don't sadly and I don't think I will when I get wherever I get to wherever it is I am going…

Sometimes you will see something, or hear something, say something or do something that you're not really sure about. Some days are good and others you have to take as life throws at you.

When we react to things some people over react, they over do it, when really sometimes we should all say, "Hey, shit happens." And then just get on with life, why waste time giving in and knuckling under, when you could be quite happily be enjoying yourself.

It's what life is really for. Life is here to be enjoyed and to be lived, as it were to the best you can. I mean there is no point in living if you can't feel alive is there now?

And should you choose to make it easy on yourself, or challenge the way you live, and struggle day by day then I take my hat off to you all, as life may be described as a rollercoaster or game we all play, but in whatever way we look at life it is in my opinion, well what was it I said now? Oh yes I remember now...

"LifE Is A Two Letter Word."

Now let me break that down for you, because what you miss the first time will now become all too clear. Life is full of IF's, quite literately, you see the word LIFE is spelt L, I, F, E... so in the middle of the L and the E we find the word IF.

And that makes LIFE a two letter word, not a two word, word. That just doesn't sound good, but Life being a two letter word sounds much better and can make a whole load of sense in the middle of it all, and unless I'm much mistaken that is what we've been talking about...The Middle.

It's not such a riddle after all, and life can be easy, it's not always swell, tell the truth every now and then or does the truth hurt like hell?

Now I'm almost at an end with this, because I may not tell you the truth. The whole truth and nothing but the truth come the next chapter which is all about Lying, this then flows through to Living and Losing...

Three parts that should flow quite nicely if I get it just right, but when I think about it I haven't really got all of the middle covered yet...

Now admit-tingly when I sat here early evening one Sunday after volunteering with the RSPB at Lincoln Cathedral, there are a pair of nesting Peregrines on the south side of the main tower, they have been there three years. They had two chicks this year, and they are quite a sight to see.

Sorry digressed a bit there, but what I'm getting at is that life often digresses and we find ourselves stuck with something or someone or even one of those glitches that seems to happen as if by magic it comes at us out of nowhere...

And that's what took place here, quite strangely in the middle of it all I nearly forgot what I wanted to write, or why I should call this chapter 'The Middle' after all.

Was it because there are ten chapters in this book and this is number five, but if you count from zero, then is five the real half of ten? And how do write zero in roman numerals?

Spot the silly question? You can't write zero in roman numerals, there is no character for it, if you had nothing to show, then a blank space was left, but if you had one or two things then the number of things you had was written beside your name...

I considered showing you what that might look like for a second just then, but then reconsidered, I may be an idiot, but I do not take the reader of this book for one.

No offence should ever be taken by anything in this book by the way, so I apologise if you have already read something you found to be offended by. And should anything else come up that you take offence to, then apologies again.

However there is in some respect a need to offend a reader of a certain book, if you read gritty thrillers or sexy romantic books, some people would find either or both to be offensive.

I find some books about the role of the man in certain aspects and parts of his body to be offensive, just as I have known women to be offended at the way they have been represented in books, or they are just an object of sex, deceit and even murder…

All things considered then the middle of anything is quite often the best of times and the worst of times, even though when we were teenagers we thought life was good, and yet it could have been bad. In some ways it is often all downhill as life goes on, but don't sit here and get yourself down.

Look to the brighter side of things, by now even if you're at forty and not done some of those things you wanted to do by now, don't panic, you've easily got another forty years to do them all, well I hope you have.

You see the middle of life is most likely going to be half way through it, and if you think you've got nothing to show for it then you're not really thinking that hard at all.

This is the middle, you can enjoy life still, and who ever said you couldn't? I mean if I get to be older, and I hopefully I will, then I look forward to being thirty, it's now only less than four years away…

So if your already forty or just about there, then look forward to it, has you were only twenty-one once and you'll only be forty once, life does after all go on.

We get through the middle of things easier and quicker often more than when we were teenagers, some of that youthful energy may have gone, but we are wiser, we are more adapt than the youth of today, we can do things we only ever dreamt of when we were young.

If you have children, you get to play the parental role now and you can ground that moody teenager when they stroll in at two in the morning, despite being told to be home at ten, never mind the fact that you did it at there age...

Now we are older, now we are in the middle of at all and we will have lived a little, we will have lied and we will have lost but we will still have life in us.

So hold on for the rollercoaster ride through the next three chapters.

Because as we close the middle and I leave you to go make a cup of tea, and maybe have some of those biscuits you like or the ones left over from Christmas. I guess it all depends on what time of year it is doesn't it?

Now what was the next chapter? Was it a pink elephant, a trip to mars or a fish that weighed thirty pounds and was 'this' big?

Only I'd be LYING if I said that the butler did it....

LYING

Lying is the most different thing that we humans do from all other animals, a dog does not lie. A cat nor rat, nor bat or tiger can ever tell you a lie. They just can't do it.

We are the only animals that can lie, humans are the only ones on this planet that lie, and I guess the first question should be is WHY?

Now most people lie to hide something, but there are those white lies we use to save peoples feelings. So if I bake a cake and you don't really like it, but say you do because you are my friend, and you don't want to upset me after all do you now.

Lies inevitably get out of hand and some will be so fantastic, so simple and perfect that everyone has now forgotten the original lie.

If I told you that you should never believe me or never leave me and never love me the way I love you, then I would be asking a lot for you to do, and we often ask one another to do something that we can find hard to do. Lying is hard to do.

I haven't thus far lied to you in this book, and I do not intend to, but all works of Fiction are just that, a lie. Sadly a deer called Bambi, or a yellow bear and tigger the talking tiger did not exist in reality… But the story was actually quite good and even though we know it not to be true, we enjoy it never the less.

We can use our imagination to create a different world, different characters. I myself have written a couple of play's that are completely fictitious. This book then is not one big lie, and it is not one big truth, sadly it is in the shades of grey…

Yes there are shades from Black to White, which are in some way grey. Lies are what they are; they are not the truth, a shade above this lie is added to a truth or an exaggeration to a truth that does not make it a full lie, so…

"My car is fantastic! It goes from naught to sixty really fast"

Now even though I don't have a car at present, if I did there is no real lie in saying that it was fast, even if it were really slow. Do you get me?

Sadly if you do not, it's something that you'll figure out later on in life, nothing to be done about it now, and if your thinking, well I've never told a lie in my life…

You may well be wrong, if you have a younger brother or sister and you ended up making a mess one wet miserable day, and then decided that mum would tell you off for making a mess, so you blame your little sister or brother… Right?

Well I'm not saying I did, and I'm not saying you should've, but we will, if we have not already done so, we will tell at least one lie in our life time, weather we meant to our not.

Some lies we will tell for the sheer need to lie, some lies will be to save ourselves embarrassment, other lies used to hide things or protect things…

Now I was pondering if I should tell you a lie now, or ask someone to tell me a lie, but sometimes it's not that easy, to just be able to lie…

I guess for a spy they lie to save their lives sometimes. Now that must be about the most justifiable lie, a lie to save your life.

Lying in a Court of Law is a crime and so is lying to a police officer, so try not to lie to the law, it may backfire on you.

And when a lie goes wrong, it goes wrong…

We hate it when people lie to us, we have to try to ask why they lied to us, what was the reason, and was it really worth it after all that?

Hard questions are often faced by those of us that have lied to someone, and when we are discovered it all goes 'tits up', to coin a phrase...

I should've put in a little bit about odd sayings there are maybe they'll turn up later on. For now I feel like lying to you, because I've just won one billion pounds on that quiz show off the television with Chris Tarrant… want some?

Well sadly you can't have any, because you can't win a billion pounds on that show, all you get at the top end of the scale of money is a mire million, but then if you've not got much too start off with then a million or even a grand is better than nothing.

But lying is an art form to some people it is an opportunity to escape the world they are in. It is a chance to deceive money from others or take things by deception.

Lying is a crime in one way, different to than it being for a good reason.

So is there such a thing as a bad truth?

Well it's funny we say that, as there must be a bad truth, like telling the wife her bum does look big in that dress after all, or that you had an affair last night with her sister.. Some truths hurt, they are bad truths.

So we have good truths and bad truths, good lies and bad lies and somewhere in the middle simplicity, no bad lies, no bad truths, no lies that will hurt someone when they are discovered.

So how do you hide a lie, and when does a lie become a secret?

Secrets are often not lies, but they can be in a strange sense, after all if you saw a married man kissing another woman, not his wife. It was a passionate kiss, a long deep, sensual kiss, and then his wife asks you do you think that her husband is seeing someone else? And you say no….

Is there any harm in that, you're keeping the truth from her, that you saw her husband kissing another woman…

But was it just a one off, was it a case of mistaken identity, sadly you have to ask the husband now, tell him what you saw…

You get caught up in the lie, and anyone who lies to you brings you into the lie, you then are lying every time you see someone else. It's like this:-

'John just got a new job as a tax collector. He enjoys his work and the money is good, but he cannot face the stigma that comes with his job, so he tells his friends and family that his new job is as an assistant to a Company Manager. Not too far from the truth as he is a Deputy Manager in the locale Tax collection office.

Everyone he meets he tells the same story, he works for TC Limited a small private business, they manage money and assist other companies with their money handling.

If you met John and asked him what he did for a living, he would say he was a deputy manager at TC Ltd, and then if an hour later you're in a bar and a girl who likes John asks you. "What does John do for a living? You'd reply "He works for TC Limited, they're like a finance company or something, and he'll tell you more."

You've then just lied and you do not even know it.

That's how easy it is to lie, to be caught up in a lie, to not realise that you're lying right now. I wonder if from this I can get you to lie for me so that when someone asks you about this book you tell them that it is very strange, but I guess your beginning to work that out now for yourself.

And if you are not, do not worry, carry no regardless, and say to anyone who has not read this book that it came with a free five pound note…

See what happens, because there are of course without a doubt those funny lies we tell, I did it to my little brother once. He had missed the football score between Manchester United and another team, I told him that Man Utd had lost sadly, and he believed me, right up until he checked the scores for himself…

The look on his face was a real hoot, he was not happy to hear that his lovely football team had lost. Heaven forbid that Man Utd has ever lost a football match.

No offence to any football fans, but sport involves the odd lie, just as life does.

For the lies that amuse us are those daft lies like telling your kids about the monster in the cupboard where you hide all your chocolate and sweets and biscuits, it is a method of prevention to stop them going into the cupboard and eating all the sweets and chocolate. Another method of prevention would be to put a lock on the cupboard or just simply move the items of temptation to another cupboard…

Only the sheer fun and joy of lying in a funny way is too hard to resist in some cases.

These are the lies that make us laugh and make us cry.

The dictionary I'm using to check on certain words has written in it, that the word Lie means:

Lie: (A noun) A statement that the person who makes it knows it to be untrue.

Lie: (A verb) Tell a lie or lies, be deceptive.

Lie: (Another verb) Be or get in a flat or resting position. And we do not want this term of lying, we are not lying as in lying down on the bed, we are lying as in the sense that he was lying through his teeth...

We are then in fact all lying at some point in life. And we have been lying for a few years now, probably since we first began to talk, did not Adam and Eve try to hide the fact that they did not eat from the tree of forbidden fruit, I mean why did God put the tree of forbidden fruit there in the first place?

But let us not get into a debate about religion our crime, or anything other than lying for now, as that is what this chapter is meant to be discussing, it is meant to be about the lies we have told and the ones we are about to tell.

If you lie a lot then I guess it would be nice to have a pound for every time you told a lie, but you'd have to give back ten to a hundred for everyone that hurt someone.

So lying is a bum deal nine times out of ten, and that is often the way life goes.

For lying often tears life apart, and lies sometimes hold it together, without lies we just wouldn't be human, is it then in our nature too?

Who told the first lie I wonder, was it the caveman coming back late to the cave one night with nothing more than a small rabbit for tea and saying that he had tried to capture a large hare, but failed….

Or was it an early Egyptian, who had gone to buy some goods and was cheated at the market, so on his or her return home they claimed they got the best deal, if not a better deal than anyone else.

And surely when we got our first legal system's a whole load of lies would have begun to take place.

And in Law there is the opportunity to lie, there is a need to lie, and even though the risk of lying will land you in hot water (Trouble) some people will run the risk.

If a lie is worth telling then tell it well, try to keep it simple, do not say things you might forget, as being able to remember what you said is part of a great lie. The other part is to have a straight face, a cool look, a calm voice, and a strong belief in that what you are saying is in fact the truth.

If after all you believe the lie to be true, then you can then convince anyone else that you are indeed telling the truth.

Only some lies should never be believed, you should never get too caught up in the lie as it will in time bring hardship and pain.

Now I have told one or two lies, I have had lies back fire on me and I have got caught up in a lie only for it all to fail and for it all to go down in flames…

Now I could tell you an example, and I could lie… Either way, what reason would you have to believe me?

And belief is a huge part of a bigger picture, I mean if you believe the lie, and you believe something you can't see or touch, but you talk to, only it does not talk back, so then what is belief? If it is not sometimes a lie…

If I told you that you now have to believe that I have been to Amsterdam, but I did not go to the Red Light area, I did not go to those brown café's or go to Anne Frank's house. Would you believe this? Could you believe this?

I mean I have honestly been to Amsterdam, I have not yet visited Anne Frank's house, but I have gone down the Red Light area, see I lied a little, I lied to you and even though there are no more lies in this 'Run Of The Mill' book.

You will find yourself questioning whether or not you have lied, or if you have been lied to.

Because sometimes it's just so easy to tell you that black is white and white is black…. Or black is black…..

A lie can be made up on the spot, it does not matter what you say, you are indeed lying and that is the whole point of it, you want to hide the truth, you want to be able to distract the person you are lying to.

You need the lie to sound good and to be good, but it is to a cruel ending and a hard truth that makes you lie.

And lying takes over some people, they do all they can to live the lie, to be the lie, and to have everyone else believe and trust in that lie to.

Lying is one of those things that make us human. It is part of our lives. It will happen to us all at some point, for to go on living on this planet having never come across a lie…

Well I would say it was impossible.

Little lies and big lies, good lies, bad lies, lies that make you feel better or worse.

Sadly any lie, is just a lie at the end of the day, it is not the truth and it never will be.

Now I'm not saying you should now suspect everyone of lying, but be careful and if it sounds too good to be true, then you can bet it is.

Try not to lie as much as you do and next time you lie to someone, ask yourself why you lied to them, and if it'll be a lot easier to put your hand up and say, sorry I just lied to you. Then do it…

For anyone who admits lying is at least trying to save embarrassment for later and they are saying sorry for the lie too.

But I'm fed up with lying, I've got bored with all the lies we have, the lies we believe, like the lie of how we are not really damaging the planet, but in fact we are.

So let us forget lying, let us consider the here and now the time we should all be…

LIVING

Now the four little pictures should represent parts of living, the sofa I guess is one thing we would all be wise to as that thing we sit on to watch the television, or for other purposes the sofa is one thing most of us will have come across in our lives thus far.

The female explorer with the two children, not only represents motherhood, childhood and the exploration of life itself, but the journeys we all take the places we go, and the instructions we often follow. Look closer and you will see that the women is pointing, and the children paying attention, even if we do not see their faces, there is a sense that they are looking at the women holding the map…

So the person with the plans surely represents the plans we all make, but they are in the construction industry, note the hard hat. Well this would represent the humble home...

Lastly the car is for the use of transport, the joy of driving and how technology is involved in the process of living. And Living is all shown in one way or another through those four pictures, I have missed out a few other aspects to living, but let us hope we can now take a look at the way we live, and what living is to us.

When I say 'us' I sort of mean me and those people that I know, as the way I live will not be the same to the way you live, but we do all share a few qualities of life together.

You breathe in air, your heart beats and your mind thinks. You can I hope talk, read and write. Maybe you drive, maybe you go to work, and maybe you watch television…

Well so do I, now living is no coincidence, as we are all alive, but the life of humans is so different from any other animal, it's a wonder we are not the daft ones. I mean if you had to live as a dog, or a spider, how would that life be compared to your own.

What I'm trying to say is that even we humans live differently to each other but Lions live the same as any other Lion, and so do many other animals.

Dogs can live differently to other dogs, but this is because of Humans. Any domestic Animal will live different to that of a wild one, just as Lion in a zoo will live differently to that of a Lion in the wild…

Now even though I just said that a Lion lives just like any other Lion, I meant wild ones only of course, but it should be noted that I am not an expert on this, but as a rule of thumb I should be right.

And if I am wrong, then you'll have to forgive me I'm afraid, just as if you have found anything else wrong in this book, any miss-spelt words, well I should have got them all when I used spell checker, grammar is a different subject, as I have written this as best as possible. I may not be that good at English Grammar, but I'm writing this the way I want it to be, so tough look if there are some deliberate mistakes, for example each time you see the phrase that is of course quite simply put 'Run Of The Mill' then grammar say's I should put a lower case O and T, but I want capitals so I've put capitals and told the grammar checker to ignore it…

I like the idea that this is not quite 'Run Of The Mill' but then it could be in some strange way, just as living can be odd at times. So is this book and life it seems can have a few odd things about them so here are…

SOME ODD THINGS IN LIFE

When your waiting for a bus and two come along, or as you go for the bus stop a bus will go by and as you wait it seems to take hours for a bus to come along, when really you only waited twenty minutes.

You see someone you know, so stop to say hello, you know their name and they know yours, but you both walk away without ever addressing one another by your respective first names, and it is not until a few yards down the street you recall the name of the person you just spoke to…

And I'm sure I could sit here and think of loads more and I bet you could find a few odd things that happen to you…

Only this is not living, and some would say that sitting on your bum all day watching television is no life, or playing golf, or fishing, or whatever…

What then you will appreciate is actual living is just life itself, the simple day to day stuff, the little moments that come along and give us a little joy.

When you kiss a girl, when you get wet in the rain, when you go to Spain, whenever you live your life then you are living….

Life is a mystery to me and it is possibly the same for you, after all just what are we all here for? Is this it and if I've only got ninety years or so then should I be allowed to live my life and be free.

To do what I want, when I want, with whoever I want, but I want never normally gets….

So we have to say please and thank you, we must try to stay within the laws that govern the land on which we live, we should try to interact with those that we live with and those that we do not.

We should perhaps have friends and family, a place to call work and a place to call home. We even have from an early age items that belong to us, and anyone who says that you come into the world with nothing is actually a little bit wrong when you stop to think about it…

After all you have I hope a loving mother and father, or parents in some way. These parents I hope knowing that a child was due will have begun to prepare for your arrival and in doing so perhaps chosen a name for you, they will have got you somewhere to sleep, clothes to wear, and other items that you will need in the first few years of your life…

It is not until you have your own money, or get given money that you can then go out and buy things that you feel you need.

So is Life all about going around collecting the things we need?

If I am to be rich or poor, famous or not, criminal or law abiding…

If I am to work, then what will I do? How many different jobs could I have?

If this is Life after all then what fun I could have!

Now nobody will have all the answers I'm afraid, there will be people who will have some answers, but not all of them...

There will be people who will give you answers, but sadly you still have to decide if they are the right ones for you…

It goes the same throughout history, we have been here for billions or millions of years, no one seems to want to really find out if we were created or we evolved, no one wants to say that only one religion is the true religion…

Back before Henry the Eighth there were only about four main recognised religions. They were the Roman Catholic Church that had gone back as far as the Christian took over in Rome and there were Jews and there were Muslims...

In China, they would have had their own religion, different to that of the then western world, and as America had not yet been fully discovered it would have most likely had its own religion too...

But Henry the Eighth wanted to marry, and re-marry, he got fed up with the Pope, and he then set up the Church of England. We were all still Christians in the sense that we had Bibles just the same as those of the Catholic Church...

Now way back before Jesus came on the scene, there were Jews and Gentiles and other Religions of sorts. There were many different Gods for many different people.

I guess as none of us can go back in time we can't really say what these religions were like, we have an idea from historians who wrote about them, artefacts found in the ground and other pieces of History too.

Now all that I understand of these times is all that I learnt from History Books and from my days at school.

Now I hope that all of us got the chance to go to school, so that we might learn things that will help us to lead our lives, and I hope that your parents taught you a thing our too about life as you grew up..

And most of our early lives are just that, it is all about growing up. We are living just by growing up, by becoming the people that we are now, those early influences, the joy's and the pitfalls, the good times through the bad times and the music, film, book or person we all came in to contact with that helped shape the way we are.

And throughout life we humans make mistakes, we have so many and yet we have so few. Some of us see the mistakes we make as a painful memory, better off forgotten. Mistakes like putting sugar in someone's tea, when they don't take sugar are simple mistakes, they are easily rectified.

Mistakes like not doing your job properly could lead to all manner of problems, it all depends on the job you do, but I think you know the mistakes, just as I know the mistakes that humans make that are harder to live with...

And we often blame inanimate objects or other things for the mistakes we make. It is the computers fault or the lawnmower, the dog perhaps or someone else's…

When you next make a mistake, just say sorry, it's the best way. No matter what the mistake, at least if you are sincere in your apology, then the other people affected by the mistake will forgive you a little more than they would have done should you have blamed someone or something else.

Living then is quite easy and even though at times it will seem hard and you wish you had all those answers you were looking for; my advice is to not to waste time. Why struggle, why get yourself down in the dumps, when all you should really do is find something you enjoy abut life, and do it…

Seriously it's that easy, now I'm not saying go out and break the law or go and hurt someone, but I am saying go out and enjoy life, go see a film, or put on that music you like so much, go see a friend. Go see the world…

We live on such a large yet very small planet in some ways, and if you get the chance to go see a different part of the plant we call Earth, then do so.

I've been to Amsterdam, France, Germany and many other great places, I loved it! The thrill of going somewhere I had never been before, talking to people I had never met, taking in a different way of life to that of the one I lived.

Life will have many adventures for the more adventuress of us, and life may be dull if you're a dull person, but if that's the way you like life, then I take my hat off to you.

I mean you probably would not want to have my life, and I would most likely not want to live yours…

But we all dream of being famous or rich, if we are not all ready. We have hopes, we have desires and we have the life we lead...

So what more could we possibly want?

Now I'm sure a lot of people could answer that question, I even have my own answer to it….

I'd like to have a family, and a nice home…

And if there is anything you want please be sure to let me know, I can't promise that you'll get it, but as you read back over that question of what else do you need, then think long and hard about what it is you need, and why you need it…

Sometimes we don't even deserve the things we have, so why should we get more things is often a mystery…

But that's what Life was right, a mystery or was it what I said it was perhaps twice, if not three or four times before… Remember I said that…

"LifE Is A Two Letter Word."

Life had IF in it a lot, and from the weather being crap to music making it better, life is just whatever you make it.

You see life is not like a box of chocolates, or some other daft and weird analogy.

Life is what you make it, and it will be different for everyone.

My life as a Man is not the same as my sister's or my mother's life, just as it would not resemble your life. Life and living are never going to be the exact same for anyone. And as I just wrote that Life is different for us all must mean that it is important…

Now you could argue that many people, possibly twins have led the same lives together, but their thoughts will have been different, they will have wanted different things from time to time. Even conjoined twins will think differently, act differently and be different to everyone else.

Being different is the best thing about living….

Trust me, if you like rum and cola, and getting caught in the rain, if you like going to the seaside on a wet summer's day, if you like making love in the bathroom or playing football and getting drunk. If you like shaving and raving in a club, or going to a pub for the quiz and karaoke come and sing with me…

For life is not what it seems and living the dream is harder than you realised, just look at this book again and you will see that it's actually a good life after all.

Because you can do many things in life, you can learn to drive and fly, operate complex machinery. Type on a computer, be rich and be poor. You have many choices in life.

And if you do your best, or if you don't want to do your best, then there's nothing to worry about. If you're in jail and don't have a way out of crime, try to realise that maybe it's not worth has much as you thought it would be.

Challenges in life like finding a job or a wife can seem like hard work, and then again they can be easy as pie or just as easy as deciding what clothes to wear….

Life it would seem is a balance and complex of situations, time, talking and doing as well as having to eat, sleep and breathe.

The body functions on oxygen, food and drink, rest and relaxation, it uses energy to do some of the things we want to do, and some tasks involve more energy than others.

Sometimes in life we all need to just soldier on, for only you can do what must be done.

And when the clouds are grey and it looks like rain you just have to cope any way you can come sunshine or showers.

Because the weather will affect what you could do today, and the music on the radio will affect the mood you are in. What ever happened last night or a day a week or even a month ago, well all of these things can effect what you do today…

At the moment you are most likely reading this, and some of the day if not all of it will have gone, and if I said that for a pound to go to charity you had to hug the first person you saw tomorrow, other than anyone you live with, this would possibly effect your actions in the morning..

You will now then possibly consider. How will I know if you hugged someone? How will you know that I gave a pound to charity, or you will think something else, simply because you can think what you like…?

Something's in life just happen, they come quite easy to us all, other things take time and time is often all we have. But no matter how things come at us in life, the key thing to remember is that try your best and the rest is easy.

However in life sometimes everything seems F.U.B.A.R, and for anyone who does not know what that stands for it is Fucked Up Beyond All Repair or Recognition....

It all depends on the R, if it seems beyond repair then it don't repair it. But if it is not recognisable then the R should stand for Recognition. Either way it is Fucked Up...

And sometimes in Life it will seem that something's are F.U.B.A.R, but often they are far from it, and sometimes they are very close to it in some cases.

We live in a country with poverty and problems that some people are oblivious to and in other countries we see them clearly.

In Living our life we take in to account the place we live the job we have and money we need to buy things and live our lives. So if we have no money then life is hard, and if we have little food we starve.

Take into account that someone somewhere is most likely worse off than you and it may for a moment make you feel better, but if you are right at the bottom of the crap pile then this is surely the place where no one else is worse off than you.

Some ways of living are better than others, but if we ever get to a point where everyone can live equally, then I wonder what the world would be like, you see it has never happened in the past.

Through the dawns of time there has always been the lowest of lows and the highest of highs.

A King lived like a king and peasants lived like, well peasants.

In living our lives we will be playing the game of life however we can, and however it comes to us.

Because Life is possibly a game that we are all playing. Some of us want to win something and some us just want to get by and some will lose out. But do we not all lose out in the game of life when it comes to death?

But life goes on regardless and we are all heading in the same direction, some quicker than others, some are closer than others, and when it gets to that point near completion we will have all experienced one cruel thing about life and that my friends is the subject of...

LOSING

All of us will lose one thing or another in our life, and to someone who thinks differently, I would like to know how you live a full life without losing anything at all…

From losing your childhood or favourite toy, to losing friends and family when someone dies and losing a family pet to things like losing money and your virginity…

We will then have lost many things by the time we get to twenty...

And when I say lost, I mean never to be returned, I got lost has a child once, but through asking a local policemen I was able to find my mum…

So losing items like money through gambling will count as a lost never to be returned, even if you gamble again and win some money, you will have lost money before…

And when gambling that is the risk you take, win or lose.

When it comes to losing a friend, if they are not dead, there is the chance of being reunited at some point, but it will take effort and time.

So losing is actually losing something that cannot be found, won't be found or be returned to you at any point in your life. Whenever you lose something it will affect you in many different ways and we will come to that right after I realise it would be best to get the daft question out of the way nice and early and you may guess what it is going to be….

Even though I have not yet asked it, you could be thinking to yourself just as I was thinking to myself, "What have I lost recently?"

So I want you to really think now, just stop for a second as I pose the question to you, especially if your twenty, if you're not quite twenty try this anyway but just do Five years, and if you're double or triple the age of twenty then just do the last ten years...

My question is of course, if you could replace everything you had lost, if you had kept a record of everything and everyone that you had lost in the last ten years...

Then what would be on that list, how many things would there be?

Would you have lost say? :-

A: Ten things.

B: Fifty things?

C: A hundred things or

D: More?

Now if you only lost ten things in the last ten years, then lucky you. If you lost more than a hundred, or you thought actually I lost that, but found it again…

It's hard I know and although I did not do it myself, the simple thing was that even if I did the last year it would take a lot of concentration and recollection to recall all the things I had lost in that year, let alone the last five or ten.

Now if I lost some money through gambling, I would not be too bothered, I decided to risk my money that way and I was not lucky enough to win, so it is my own fault.

Now I'm not condemning gambling, but people do get addicted to it, they lose thousands of pounds and get into huge debts, and it is the same with any addiction...

Addiction to alcohol or drugs is often a bad thing. They take over your life and will often ruin it.

I have found that people addicted to drugs, drink or gambling have more to lose, and they often lose it all.

"When it's gone it's gone."

Losing a limb or your sight, or part of your own body is not the same as losing your way whilst going for a walk, or losing five pounds because one football team beat another…

Losing time is not the same as losing a loved one to cancer or death. Losing your licence because you were drunk and over the limit is not the same as losing a pound on the lottery, if you took a life whilst you were drink driving, you now have to live with the fact that you have caused someone to lose someone.

Sometimes when we lose things like the lottery or quiz's, well that is an acceptable loss, just like when you play a computer game and you lose, or when you run a race and come last…

Losses like this are often quite easy to except, but if you lose a friend or family member in a car crash caused by a drunk driver, this loss can be hard to bear or cope with.

Other personal losses like to those we love and have our first sexual encounter with. (When you lose your virginity) Well this loss should be with your consent, and you should want to lose your virginity, be happy to lose your virginity and feel good once your virginity has gone.

Losses like losing at strip poker, or a promotion at work, a moment of time or a tooth. These losses can seem small, they can be fun and they can provoke a question or two.

If you lose out at work, if you lose a day's pay, or lose time in traffic then you will ask why? You will want to know why you did not get promoted or get extra work at the weekend, you will know you were ill, or your child was ill so you could not go into work so you lose a day's pay and as the train lines or accident slowed the traffic down this is the reason why you lost that moment in time.

So losing has its excuses, it has its up's and it has its down's….

I'd like to look at one particular loss, a small loss, a silly loss that I think might just be used to help explain much larger losses, it won't help for every loss but, it will help you realise that if it's easy to lose this and you do not feel the loss, then the loss of something ten times bigger will I hope seem the same as this loss.

In the case of a life, you will be able to recall the good times, and even though they are lost to you through death, in fact the memory of that person lives on in you and the memories of those that knew that person too.

You will forget the loss, you will see the loss in a whole new way, and hopefully when you lose something again, you'll go back to this book and get to this point and say to yourself.

"Well I've just dropped an egg on the floor! It is lost, it is gone, it is of no use, it just remains to be cleaned up and then it is gone, but I wanted to fry it and have a sandwich. It was my last egg, I have no more. Silly me, oh well never mind

I've got a banana here instead, much better for my health than a fried egg sandwich."

Now think about it, it was just an egg, and although it is daft to compare this to losing a pet dog, because he was too old and had to be put down, well it is not exactly the same.

What I guess you have to realise is that if the dog is so old that the only option to save the dog a long and painful death is for the dog to be put down, then this is what you do. You also I hope will have photo's of the dog, you will consider getting a new one, not to replace the dog you had, but to at least help with the loss.

It's the same with the last egg, I can easily go and get more, and although I can't get another person when one dies. I can at least remember them.

When your friend or family member dies, this is the loss that will be the hardest to cope with and sadly I'm not an expert in telling you how to cope with it, but you might want to try the egg thing out for a laugh.

Think about the egg's journey to you, the time it was sat in the fridge or wherever you kept it, think about what you knew the egg could be used for, soon you will see that the ability to recall those good times, the laughs you had with your dead friend or family member is of some comfort at least.

And losing things like life or money or promotion at work to losing days, months and years can all go back to the loss of that egg.

When we lost the egg through dropping it on the floor, our initial thoughts are most likely to be "Clumsy me!" or "Dam! I have to clean that up now, and I only cleaned the floor yesterday."

We think to ourselves, "I was looking forward to that fried egg sandwich, now what am I going to have?"

Do we consider going to the shops to get more eggs, or do forget it and have something else. Like the banana…

Now those parts at least can be used when it comes to some losses, like when we lose money by gambling, and when we lose some time to.

When we lose things that can be replaced, we will most likely replace them. If we lose things through crimes like burglary and theft, we hope that the criminal will be caught and punished. And possibly we will get back some of the things they took that belonged to us.

If you are a virgin and raped, then getting your virginity back won't happen, but I hope that the person who raped you will be dealt with by the authorities.

So some losses can be regained they are not at all worthless loses, like that in a game of chess.

You see a worthless loss is that of playing any board game, there will be a winner and there will be a loser, if you lose, do so with grace and pride. There is nothing worse than a sore loser when it comes to playing a game.

Most of the things we lose we are not worried about, other losses in life will cripple us, they will upset us and they will seem like we lost everything we had.

Only you don't lose everything you have until it's all gone and you are dead.

And we will come to death a little later, but for now we are alive, there is a sense that we can do anything we put our minds to, we could climb Mount Everest, go to see a film at the locale cinema, go to the shops for more eggs, learn to drive, learn a new language and do many other great things…

But are there things that a man cannot do that women can, and things that women cannot do, but men can?

I guess child birth is the key thing about what women can do, but men cannot.

I wouldn't even say that if a man had a sex change to become a woman, he could have children right away. There must be a process for a man that has become a woman to go through for them to have children, if it is at all possible.

A woman can't really play with her penis, and a man can't play with his vagina…

In days gone by women were not allowed to do certain jobs, and I think men could not do some jobs that women did too.

Nursing springs to mind, it would've be in years gone by a job for a woman and not a man…

Now let us not be sexist, but let us remember the fact that all women did not get the vote until 1919.

You see what I'm saying is that some men will have said back in 1919, that it was uncalled for or that the country would go in to ruin now that women could vote, but they were wrong, you see it's democratic for women to be allowed to vote, I think when you get to sixteen you should be allowed to vote, as not enough young people tend to vote…

And that is a loss to anyone! If you have the chance to vote at the next elections then you should.

Because changes happen, they happen for good and they happen for bad, but change happen.

And changes in the lies we tell, the way we live and how we lose will all have been part of our lives.

If you have lost something then you will know the pain felt by the loss, the stupidity of the loss, or the sheer hassle of the loss.

Because different things that are lost to us will always affect us differently, just as the loss of millions of men as they went over the top on July first nineteen sixteen, the first day of the battle of the Somme.

The loss of these men is nothing in comparison to losing your mobile phone, just as any recent losses in Afghanistan cannot be compared to the banks losing all that money.

Both the loss of soldiers in Afghanistan and the loss of money in poor Icelandic investments have affected this country in different ways this year, 2009.

And what of our losses, should we try to forget them all? When we look back at my 'egg' theory, you may think I forgot that to completely forget the loss of the egg and move on as if it did not happen was incorrect. Especially in the case of the loss of those soldiers or civilians who have died in any war.

However when you reconsider the fact that wars are often caused by one country invading another, or by religion or by terrorism or however they are started…

The 'egg' as it were, will be broken during the conflict, it is expected that someone will lose out whilst the war takes place, how we recover from the loss is the more important thing to think about.

Losing can be fun, some people set out to lose certain things, and others set out to win.

Wining a war will have advantages and disadvantages, you will have had to pay for the war, and you will need people to have fought in the war, so all parties involved will lose many things during the war.

In war there are battles and even though battles can be won and lost, there are times when all the battles can be won, but the war is lost....

Losing is all a part of the bigger picture sometimes; small losses will not influence the eventual outcome. The loss of supplies, life in low numbers and even intelligence can sometimes be thrown away as part of the bigger picture to win a war. Were as other losses, such as huge losses in life and supplies or other tactical advantages will eventually cause many a problem for all concerned in war.

Because sometimes we can't always win, we must be prepared to lose in any way that a loss comes.

And as we lose the things we hold dear as we get closer to losing everything

After all: "One minute you're here and the next you could be gone."

If we do lose out in death, then maybe we have nothing to lose in death, but then again will we not leave behind those that we loved, and the things we had accumulated in life.

I heard once that Living was in the way we die…

And in death we lose everything including our life, and who's going to tell you when it's too late? For once something is lost in life it is often very rare that we get it back.

So be thankful if you find something important that you happen to lose, and don't worry if you don't win the lottery or if you happen to misplace some money…

For to lose something and never find it, you must except that it is lost and shall not return, just as if you are fortunate for the thing that you have lost to come back, or be returned to you, then you should I guess be thankful.

Only there is of course one thing we all lose, and that is this LifE we have, and as far as I can see you don't get it back, or another one...

So you see there are bigger things in life that you will lose, and your life will be one of them, but before we lose it all, we must consider the preparation for death.

You see for some people the end is near and for others it is far away, only to be honest I can't say when the end will come for anyone, including me…

So you have to live life to full and when you think the time is getting near then I guess you will in some strange way be…

GETTING READY TO GO.

Where are we getting ready to go?

On holiday? To the shops? Death perhaps, as we reach sixty or seventy or if we are lucky enough to get to a hundred…

Only is life at the age of sixty to eighty all about getting ready to die, or should we still be able to have the rest of lives lived out to the full?

I'm not quite yet seventy or eighty for that matter. It is a long way off, somewhere in the distance it waits for me, but should I be ready to go at any point, and how do I know if I'm ready to go when the time comes?

You see this chapter will not only now get you thinking, but it will also if you are in those years close to a natural death perhaps start to get you to wonder about death itself.

Because if death can happen in a flash and you could be gone before you finished the end of this book! Not only is that a scary thought, but you have to consider, what is there to do before I go?

Is there anything we can do before death to prepare us for it, or should we have tried to do as much with our life as we wanted to do before we die?

Death is the end of life, after death no one really knows what will happen, some believe that there is a heaven and a hell, others say there is nothing after death and some think that there is something, but they do not know what.

I was once led to think that anything after this life on earth would surely be better than the life on earth I have had.

Only that depends on the life you have had, if you consider your life to have been good or worthwhile, then why would you want anything better when you are dead?

If on the other hand you think that you have wasted your life then surely you are to blame the most for this, as there are many things you can do in life if you put your mind to it and you try, try and try again.

If at first you do not succeed, do not give in, have another go!

You see the prospect of death throws in the subject of my next chapter, but we're not quite ready to talk about when it's all gone, we'll come to that a hundred pages from now….

A little lie there for you, as there will most likely be about six or seven pages in this chapter and then when it's all gone the book will be finished. I'll have to ask someone to read it through, get there opinion and then get it published.

I'm then getting ready to go, and I'm writing this book as a jovial look at life, a look at the things we do that make us human. We watch films, we play games, we lie, we cheat, we love and we lose.

We will all die naturally, or in war, by accident, by murder or in some other cruel way, but we will all day one day. Perhaps as this book draws to an end I wanted to pose a thought on it to save you having to pose a thought about it…

After all Humans think and talk, they sell, they buy, they build and they destroy, they love and they lose, they win and they fight. We go to war, we listen to music, we fly and we drive and survive by farming other animals and plants.

We waste things and we use things, we have phones and we have clothes. We try to get by on the money we get, we go on holiday and we go to see family and friends.

Sometimes it all depends on the weather, but no matter what we are all human at the end of the day, and some are happy and some are sad, some are somewhere in the middle of it all and others are getting ready to go far away from it all.

When you're ready to go, I hope you will have had a good life. You will have done as much or as little as you wanted to do, you will be happy that you did your best and you got through life the best way you knew how…

You lived your life to the full; you were free to be whatever you wanted to be…

And now the time is here and you are ready to go, but what did you to do to be ready to go in the first place?

I mean is there any real way to be ready for death?

You see I don't think there is any reel way of preparing for death, you can accept the fact that you will die one day and that day could be tomorrow or it could be far away in the future.

Some of us know when we will die, we can expect it soon if we are terminally ill, if we are very old and frail, and struggle day by day to live, then death it would seem is closer to us than we think.

This goes for the healthy and young, as you can be careless and get run over whilst crossing the road, you could be out one night and get hit by a drunk driver. You could be shot, especially if you are a soldier at war.

So death is closer to some of us than others and to those that do not see death coming anytime soon, then do not worry. There are better things to do in life than worry about death.

If you do see death just around the corner, then do not worry either, as it is the end of your natural life, and remember you have had fun and enjoyed your life thus far. Even if you think that you haven't…

Just think that even if you were poor, or you could not do what you wanted to do with your life, then what does it matter? Surely there was one occasion in your life when you enjoyed it?

Life is worth living, so make sure you live as much as you can before you go, try not to worry too much and if you are able to live day by day or week by week then lucky you.

Some people let the years roll by, they just admire life. There is not that much too it after all. Only more fool them, because there are many wonderful things in life that we can all do.

Only if this is the only life you are going to get then if you can do something with it, anything at all, anything in your power then you should at least try to do it.

Don't forget:-

"LifE Is A Two Letter Word."

It is often the 'IF's' in life that get us through. It is the "IF's" and the maybes or the who, what, when, where, why and how of life that we all have to cope with and live with…

Life is life and nothing changes it unless you change it. Sure, there'll be people who will want you to change your life and there will be people you change your life for, but you make all your own choices past the age of thirteen to eighteen, and it all depends really on those little choices you made as child. Only you were not fully aware of them at the time.

Simple choices like what to wear, or where to go, what to eat and when to eat…

Difficult choices like what job to do, or who to kiss and when to kiss them.

Choices are the best part of being Human other than life and living itself.

Getting ready to go isn't easy, you have to consider the things you have collected during your life, as sadly you can't take them with you when you die. Well I don't know of anyone who has managed to take things that they had in their life with them into death…

So you need to write your "Last Will and Testament", a legal document to say what you want to happen to those things that belong to you, and you decide if you want to be buried or cremated.

If you have very little or if you have lots, if you have a large family or you have no one at all, deciding who gets what when your gone is I guess a hard thing to decide.

It is a difficult choice to make, but one that will not bother you when you are dead, well at least I don't think it will.

And when it comes to those late stages of life, if we are in a care home, then I think the process of getting ready to go is easier in some way as the place you are in now is the last you shall live in before you die.

Some people get to die in their own home, others die in a care home, and others die in war or by the roadside. Some die in hospital and some die in a far way country.

Death then is everywhere just the same as life. It seems that the three real things that seem to be everywhere we go are LIFE, DEATH and THE WEATHER.

Only there is no weather on the moon, but not all of us will get to go there, and if anyone lands on Mars or Pluto. Well I'm sure I won't be able to go and neither will you most likely.

And if you can go to Mars or Pluto, if you have the opportunity to do anything before you die, then I would encourage you to do it.

If it involves breaking the law, then I would discourage you from doing it, but if it is legal, then go ahead. Enjoy life before it is over…

We can do anything really, we can fly far away, we can go around the world and back again, we can eat chocolate, watch films and play the game of life until it comes to an end…

We can be pretty much anything we want to be, some men become women and some women become men, we are able to do so much with so little time, it would be near impossible to do it all.

I'd love to go swimming with Dolphins or go to the Islands of Japan. I'd like to see Niagara Falls and the Pyramids...

So much to do and so little time, but time can be made to do the things you want to do, because you must have made time to read this book, or this page, and you'll have time to go and get a cup of tea, a beer or a beverage if you want one.

Making time to do the things we want in life can be hard at times, it will cause conflict with other things, but it will be beneficial to us all when we do make time to do what we want.

Time then is of the essence is it not, but time goes by slowly and yet it can just disappear as if it were not there at all sometimes.

We all, I guess have had those slow days sat at home thinking of things to do, and those days when we rush around like a headless chicken.

We long for some days to be over and for some to begin, we wait for some days to come and we don't mind the day's that have gone.

You see waiting for your exam results after doing your GCSE's or University Degree is a long process from the last exam in May right through to mid August. The wait is long, but it soon comes around and there they are the grades that determine how qualified you are and what you'll do next in life.

Sadly death is not like getting ready to go to school, or to work or go on holiday.

Getting ready to go anywhere at the best of times will often take some effort and some time to organise as well as prepare for where you want to go.

Sometimes all the best laid plans go to ruin or rest. And by that I mean that even if you meticulously plan your journey or trip to your destination, there are always going to be a few unseen things that might happen along the way.

The weather could change, the traffic could be bad, and you could forget something or see someone on route and get distracted.

Lots of things can affect the plans we make, but every now and then the plans we make just seem to go off without a hitch.

The plans that are best laid to rest or the ones that we dream of, the ones we would like to do, but will most likely not get the chance to do them.

And not having time to do all those things can seem annoying, but if there is just one thing that you could do, and say for arguments sake you could do it right now….

Insert silly question here, I guess…

Come on you must now be thinking about that one thing that you could do, and you hopefully guessed that I was going to ask what it would be and give you four options to chose from., but unfortunately they may not be the right four options.

They might not be what you want to do, but they will give you an idea if I tell them to you, if I write them down right here and right now…

So go on then, if there were just one thing you could do and you could do it right now what would you chose:-

A: Go see your family or a friend you have not seen for a while.

B: Go to Paris, New York, Rome, London or Tokyo….

C: Go to the Moon.

D: None of the above. You'd rather instead I got on with the book?

And get on with the book I shall, but we are at the end or close to it, I may have not fully covered the whole process of getting ready to go, but I have talked about the ways we are ready to go anywhere and do anything in life and this includes death.

Because how can you fully prepare for death, unless you know the exact moment it will happen to you?

And so getting ready to go anywhere has its problems from the very beginning.

We have to understand that being ready to go and going aren't really the same, the fine line that separates them is hard to see, but you'll know from any experience of going anywhere that in my opinion anyway…

"There is always one more thing to do!"

And this is the case of getting ready to go, what we do when it's all gone is something else, and that is why we come to it last.

I will then move on from getting ready to go to the next chapter of…

When It's All Gone.

Now I'm not completely sure what will happen when my life is gone, that is to say when I am dead.

One thing is for sure and that is I'll be dead one day and so will you…

Only first before anything else in this chapter about 'When It's All Gone' let us think about what will happen when we are dead?

Now I believe that there is a heaven and possibly a hell, but I can't go there like I could go to the Bahamas or Liverpool. Well not just yet, if we have to be dead to go to heaven, I don't fancy dying just to see if it exists.

In fact if anyone has gone to heaven, then why has no one come back and told us about it? I guess the same goes for hell, all we really know about heaven and hell is what we are told by various people throughout life.

Whether or not we listen to these people is our choice, and I guess that if there is a heaven and that the only way of getting in is to believe in it and all that this entails. I should have perhaps covered religion as topic in this book.

Only problem with that is I have found through past and personal experiences that religion over complicates the simplicity of there being a God and there being a heaven and a hell.

When Christianity took off after the death of Christ, it was simple, there was just the one church that followed Christ, but over time it became the Roman Catholic Church and then Henry the Eighth broke away from that during the reformation and the Anglican or Church of England was formed.

Then later Mormons and Methodists came into the limelight of the main role of being a follower of Christ. Baptist, this that and the other religion seemed to appear throughout history. In fact I could probably start my own religion today.

After all being a Jedi is a religion nowadays, but what about other religions?

What about the Muslims and the Jews, the old religions of the Greeks and Egyptians?

I wonder just exactly how many religions there are out there to choose from and if any of them actually believe that they are the right one when it comes to explaining creation and life and what happens when we die.

Those that do not believe in a God and those that believe in Evolution or Science can fall into the category of religion too.

Religion is the belief we have about the existence or non-existence of God.

So just thinking about the choice of religion once more can I ask you just how many religions there are? Do you think there are:-

A: Five

B: Twenty

C: Fifty

D: More than Fifty, but really about twenty-five are really Christian anyway.

Now when I say Christian I mean a follower of Christ, anyone who follows Christ is a Christian, whether they are Baptist, Methodist, Salvation Army, Catholic, Protestant or other Christian.

The only real differences are the way in which they follow Christ or how the church stands within the world today.

The biggest difference between the Catholic and Protestant church was Divorce.

If I'm right then it's mainly the fault of Henry the Eighth that the tree of religion split. From it being a solid path that led back to Christ, now there are many branches that have sprung from one original source.

So if we ever get the chance to go back in time I guess the real key time to go back to will be the birth and last three years of Christ's life.

If you were there to see him crucified, and if you witnessed the breaking of the bread to feed five thousand or Christ walking on water or any other of the things Christ did that we can only read about in one book. The Bible….

Would you believe?

The only trouble is we can't go back in time, because then we would have the opportunity to change things would we not, and if we could do this some would want to go back and kill Hitler or do other things that would perhaps upset the balance of history.

So what is done is done. What is said is said. We all do or say things from time to time that we will regret, I don't regret writing this book, I try not to regret the things I have done and the things I have said.

Sometimes when I can't think of anything to say, I think I should say nothing at all.

Words will hurt you sometimes and they can destroy you, words will empower and build you up. Words help us and hinder us, they make us Human…

Now I don't quite know how many times I have to tell you I'm sorry for any offence taken by anything in this book, but sometimes life is hard and we have to cope with hardship, it is part of life.

The best thing to do is not let it get to you. Bullies rely on the reaction of the victim, they want you to fight back, but it is often better not to give them the satisfaction.

We can all be put upon in our lives and we can all struggle with life, we can get by and we can try to do our best.

When it comes to the end of life as you have known it, I'm sure that just before you go you'll get the chance to remember some of the things you did. Perhaps you went to war, perhaps you were rich beyond belief and perhaps you had nothing at all.

You could have lived on an island or on the main land, perhaps you are white, black, Asian or another race. Maybe life was good and then again it could have been bad.

Whatever life you have had or currently having, then I hope that it is one that you are enjoying as much as you can.

If life has a purpose for you then I hope that you have been able to fulfil that purpose and do whatever it is you wanted to do.

We could have been anyone we wanted to be, we could have done anything we wanted to do…

And you will have had friends and family by your side you will have been involved in other people's lives and they will have been involved in yours.

Sometimes you will have wondered why you were mixed up in other people's lives and how they came to be mixed up in yours.

With some people I often wonder why they really need me, or talk to me, I think to myself that if I were to just leave and go far away, would they miss me?

Would anyone miss you as when we are dead we are at least gone from this earth, where we go is another question at present, but what about the things we leave behind? Well this is the topic I want to talk about first.

If you own your own home and were married but your partner is dead and has been for some time, then your house will perhaps be left to your children if you have them, even if I guess they have their own homes.

The money from the sale of the house will go somewhere, any property you had will I guess be sold as well.

It kind of begs the question of why do we in life accumulate so much, when in death it will be all gone?

The ancient Egyptians were buried with all their worldly goods believing that they would need them in the next life, slaves were killed to be with the dead King or Queen of Egypt so that in the afterlife they would have servants to look after them.

If you could be buried with all your worldly goods would you?

The only thing is that years from now someone will most likely dig them up and they will be antiques.

When DVD's are obsolete in a hundred or a thousand years from now, will they be antiques?

VHS has gone along with the record, paintings of Picasso and Monet are antique and if I were a famous painter then surely my art would become an antique a thousand years from now.

And I guess that having realised that the things we have, all be it that they are nice and make life easier, in reality we won't need them later on and we certainly won't need them in death.

The washing machine, the fridge, the television, that dress, those million pairs of shoes, your collection of stamps or train set, or car or James Bond posters. DVD's, CD's and the computer will all be no good to you when you are dead.

The only things that will remain of you are those few photo's that you are in, the memories you left in other people's minds and a tombstone if you have one.

If you are famous then the whole world will stop to remember you when you die. If you are not famous then only the people that knew you will think about the loss of you from their lives.

And losing was discussed earlier, just as any lies you told in life, now they are gone and no one will have known.

You leave it all behind in death and sadly that is the way of life.

I will leave many things behind when I am gone. One of them I hope will be this book and so to you in the year 3000. Providing that the world gets that far around.

Well to you I say hello and do you know the Music of Queen and ABBA? Have you ever seen The Shawshank Redemption and are they still making James Bond Films?

If I get to be a hundred before I die and the year is 2083, try and look me up…

I wonder what will happen in my life time. I wonder if anyone getting on the Titanic would ever have thought that it would sink.

I wonder if in 1914, just as Britain went to war with Germany anyone thought I bet we have to do this all over again in 1939…

What did Shakespeare think about life, why did Napoleon try to conquer Russia and what would the world be like now if anyone had done things differently?

Say the car had only just been invented, or the cinema or any other great invention of years gone by. How would you react?

If the ice caps melt anytime soon, did I ask you if I could borrow your boat if you have one?

Sometimes I guess we can go too far and think about too much. Sometimes we should not worry as much as we do, I bet anyone living in the times of the Romans or Vikings, or Normans never panicked as much as we do now.

It is then the human factor of imagination that deters the way in which we can escape the reality of the fact that we humans have polluted our planet, we humans would rather jet off to Mars than sort out the problems we face with hunger and drought.

All of us have an imagination and some of us have a better one than others.

I should point out that I have a great imagination. Being able to talk about it and write about it is often amusing and strikingly odd.

I'm a wonder of creation as my mind can often cause frustration, especially as I sat and I wrote this 'Run Of The Mill' book.

But I got there in the end, all one hundred pages of it, just remember though that I wrote this on a computer to start off with and when I say a hundred pages I mean one hundred A4 pages, just how many it will be when it comes to it being laid out in a 'Run Of The Mill' book style I just don't know.

Now when it is all gone I think I will be happy in the knowledge that I had a good life.

I hope that you have had a good life are you are going to have a good life. Life after all is what you make it.

Many people will come along to help you live your life and some will want you to do things and others will not.

Life is yours and yours alone. No one should try to control your life for you.

Some people need others to help them live and even though they need a helping hand in life, it is always best to remember that the life they have is theirs and if they can choose to do things they want to do and they are old enough to choose or do what they want to do then you should let them.

In life we know we have to wait from the moment we are born until we are old enough to choose for ourselves and do what we want to do.

We have to wait until eighteen in Britain to drink Alcohol and the age is twenty-one in America, fourteen in Spain and sixteen in France.

Different countries have different rules and different ways of life. And if you get the chance to go and the see theses different ways of life then do so. I did.

To go where you want to go and do what you want to do is part of life it is the freedom we have as Humans, whether it was given to us or not.

Because who gives you the freedom to do what you want, when you want?

I don't and I don't think any other human does, except for you. You have to decide if it is legal, if it is safe and what, if any or the consequences of your actions.

If God judges you in death and you have repented for all your so called sins then you can be safe in the knowledge that a place in heaven awaits you, can't you?

You see this life is the only one that you get that I know of, some people think that they have lived before, in years gone by, they believe in reincarnation.

And for anyone who wants to come back from the dead as a Tiger, dog or cat or another human then the best of luck to you.

If you die before me and get the opportunity to come and tell me what exactly happens, then this would be much appreciated.

Sorry, no offence to anyone, but knowing and not knowing could I think make life better for some people, but for others not wanting to know or just not caring is better.

Most people will go through life not really worrying about death until that is when they come face to face with it.

Some of us will look up and call out for God just like the Man who fell off a cliff and as he fell he managed to grasp a branch. No one was nearby, not another single human was within a good ten miles, and no one could help the man and the branch would not hold out should help come along. Time was running out and the rocks below meant certain death.

The man cried out, he called out Help at first, then "God?"… A voice from the clouds replied "Yes?" The man then asked the voice he presumed to be God to help him.

The voice of God said let go of the branch and I will save you. The man looked down and considered the offer before asking if anyone else was there to help…

Now I heard this story and thought to myself why did the man not let go? Why not try to climb back up the cliff? Why not wait an hour if he could and if the branch would hold his wait, surely someone might come along?

Unfortunately I've never understood what is meant by the story, if there is any moral to it all.

Don't forget what I said about life and that it I think -

"LifE Is A Two Letter Word."

And you're probably fed up of me saying it and if you have not yet figured it out or just what point I'm trying to make by saying that "LifE Is A Two Letter Word". Then let me tell you.

You see if you look at life closely you see that we in the English way of life spell it L, I F, E.

We put the word IF right in the middle of life. Now I don't know where the original word of life came from, perhaps some Latin or Greek word was first translated to English and this is where we got the word life from?

But I wonder why life, why not something else? Have you ever considered that if you had to name an animal, a cow perhaps? Would you call it a cow?

Why not a Milk Mammal? Or Wok, Milky or any other name you happen to decide upon. If your name is George, why not call it a George?

And if the man who first drank from the udder of a cow had got the bull by mistake? And why did he or she call the white stuff that came out as they 'Milked' the cow, well why did they call it milk?

Now I may have gone off the subject and I may not have, you see the big IF in life is life itself.

Sadly we don't have enough time to be able to know everything in life, I know I don't.

We can only know what we know about the past from the people who wrote about it and the things they left behind before they died.

This is what we call History and this was the lives of people who are no longer here.

So when I say that little phrase that I hope I might just get remembered for, not only am I trying to be philosophical, but I'm also trying to get remembered.

And when it's all gone some of us will be remembered and some of us will eventually be forgotten.

Sadly at the end of life comes death, although some people and some cultures may actually look forward to death.

Death could be a celebration of the life you had, it could be a time to remember all that you accomplished in life, the lives of others that you touched. A joyous occasion instead of a sad one. And if in death we can find peace and happiness then surely the life we have led will have been worth it all in the end.

I can't say what a life is worth exactly and whether or not some lives should be worth more than others, but some people do consider that there life is better than yours.

True happiness can be found in many forms to many different people and death is one thing that just as in birth we will have all had in common.

We are born, we live and we die, some die too young and some die in war or in an unforeseen accident. Some people take life through murder and sometimes death happens naturally.

No matter how or when you die, you will be dead one day and although it's a hard thing to consider, the sooner you appreciate the fact of life that it ends in death, the easier it will be to get on with your life until death comes.

So go and live your life for there are many things you can do, do you not recall some suggestions from my chapter about living? Maybe you should just flick back to see the many wonders of living before dying.

And then again maybe you feel you have led your life, or you are living your life the way you want to and why should I tell you to live it any differently.

Not that I am trying to say this is the way to live your life, if you go by my example, then more fool you, for we all need to live our own lives for ourselves.

Live your life and be free to do what you want to do and in death I hope you find what you expected, if there is anything to find.

For when it is all gone I will have lived my life as much or as little as I wanted to.

If there was anyone wanting me to do anything special with my life, then I wish that they had made this clear, after all I am just a simple human, what do I know about life other than the one that I have?

How can I be important to anything at all, and why should I be important if I don't want to be?

Why is life so easy and yet so hard, why do we cry and why do we fight one another for a piece of land or to impose a way of life on someone?

Why should others live the way we live, why should diseases like aids and cancer still exist?

Why we do what we do only we will ever know why really. We made the choice, we chose this rather than that and even the people we elect to make choices for us in Parliament can be wrong, but we elected them, all accept Gordon Brown. No one elected him to be Prime Minister.

And so in life choices are good and choices are bad, but I said that once already, what I'm trying to end on is that in reality Life is what you make it and it's entirely up to you what you do with your life before you die.

So go out and do what you please with your life, it is after all yours.

And when the pen runs out of ink, just as we run out of life, what has been written? What have we learnt? What do we wish we did not want to do, but did it anyway.

Because when it is all gone and when you and I are no longer here on earth and we are perhaps somewhere else in death or we are nowhere at all, and if we have the chance to say that we did what we wanted with our lives then surely it will have been worth it all.

To think we could have done more will only upset the balance of life, because not even I was able to do everything. When all is said and done that's it, "The End".

So fare thee well my friends and thank you for the time you have took to read my 'Run Of The Mill Book'

Authors Note

I just thought that to round things off I would have some sort of personnel note from me to you.

I hope that you have had a giggle as you read this, I hope you were not offended and I hope that you might have enjoyed reading this 'Run Of The Mill' book and next time you come back to peruse through it you'll find something you missed last time.

You'll probably try to remember some of those daft questions and you'll be trying to work some out if you really wanted to take the time to do so.

And time has been taken away from you to read this book and for this I say thank you, now don't forget to look out for other titles by myself.

So it's goodbye from me and goodbye from you, for when it's all said and done and the battle is won, who is real winner and who is the real loser?

Just remember one thing, even if it does not make sense at first, it will then I hope be one thing I get remembered for and that is that I said:-

"LifE Is A Two Letter Word."

And so with that in mind thank you once more and if your about to read the book then enjoy, it sure is more than just 'Run Of The Mill'

And these last few words just made it 32,000 words long, or there about's.

Thank you to all my readers, family and friends to Darren, Katherine, Anthony and Kimberley for their small input.

All the best.

Ed Chandler

Printed in Great Britain
by Amazon.co.uk, Ltd.,
Marston Gate.